FIVE OF A KIND

KIND BROTHERS SERIES, BOOK 5

SANDI LYNN

SANDI LYNN ROMANCE, LLC

FIVE OF A KIND

Five of a Kind

New York Times, USA Today & Wall Street Journal
Bestselling Author

Sandi Lynn

Five of a Kind

Copyright © 2022 Sandi Lynn Romance, LLC

Photo by Wander Aguiar
Model: Pat T.

❀ Created with Vellum

MISSION STATEMENT

Mission Statement

Sandi Lynn Romance

Providing readers with romance novels that will whisk
them away
to another world and from the daily grind of life – one book
at a time.

INTRODUCTION

One letter that altered my life.
A fake birth certificate.
A father I never knew about.
And four brothers who were the same age as I was.

At thirty-three years old, I was the CEO of Sterling Capital, thanks to my uncle who took me under his wing and introduced me to the world of investing. He was somewhat of a father figure since my mother never married and told me my father was a stranger she'd met in a bar.

After the sudden passing of my mother, I found out who my father really was. A man named Henry Kind, whom she had a brief affair with all those years ago. A man who left her to start a family with another woman. I was his blood, his son, and he was going to know exactly who I was when the time was right. But I needed to devise a plan to work my way into my newly found family's lives.

Buying a house down the beach from them was a start, and so was charming a beautiful woman who was close to them —a woman who was unbelievably sexy in so many ways. I'd use her to get to them, gain their trust, and take over my father's company. The one thing I didn't count on was falling for Jenni Benton in more ways than one. Then all hell broke loose after she'd found the letter my mother had left me.

I had two choices: either leave her and everything behind or stay and fight the war I started.

The thing about betrayal is that it will always come from those close to you. ~ Samuel Zulu

CHAPTER 1

*S*haun

"Oh my God, Shaun. Oh my God," Christine kept saying over and over as I had her pinned up against the wall. "Yeah, baby. Are you going to come? Are you going to come?"

I couldn't take her voice anymore, so I brought my hand up and placed it over her mouth while I continued thrusting inside her. My cock started to spasm, and with one last hard thrust, I exploded while letting out a satisfying moan. I removed my hand from Christine's mouth and placed it firmly against the wall while trying to regain my breath.

"I can't believe you covered my mouth. That was an asshole move, Shaun." Her brows furrowed.

I shook my head and lowered her down until her feet hit the floor. Walking into the bathroom, I removed the condom, tossed it in the trash, and splashed some cold water on my face.

"Hello? Did you hear me?" she loudly voiced when I walked back into the room.

"Yeah. I heard you. Get dressed." I picked up her dress from the floor and threw it at her.

"What? Why? It's one o'clock in the morning."

"I know what time it is, Christine. You need to leave." I walked over to my dresser drawer and pulled out a pair of pajama bottoms.

"Are you being serious right now?"

"Very serious." I grabbed my phone and opened the Lyft app.

"What the fuck, Shaun?" she yelled.

I left the bedroom, went downstairs to my bar in the living room, and poured myself a scotch.

"You owe me a fucking explanation!" she spewed as she followed me.

"I have a lot on my mind, and I just want to be alone tonight. Please, Christine. Don't fight me on this. A Lyft is waiting downstairs for you, and it's already paid for."

"Fine. Is there anything I can do to help you?"

"No."

I walked her to the elevator and pushed the button.

"Thanks for understanding. I'll call you." I gave her a soft smile.

"Okay. Don't make plans for this weekend. There's this great Indie band playing in Central Park I want to see."

"Sounds fun." I kissed her forehead before she stepped inside the elevator.

As soon as the doors shut, I let out a sigh, grabbed my phone, and blocked her number. Walking over to my safe, I opened it and took out the letter given to me by my mother's attorney ten days ago following her funeral.

My dearest Shaun,

If you're reading this, that means you have already laid me to rest in the ground. I know I wasn't always the perfect mother, but I tried. Growing up without a father was hard on you, and I know your Uncle Nate attempted to fill those shoes when he came back to New York, even though he had issues of his own.

There are things I'd never told you. I suppose I took the coward's way out by telling you this when I'm dead and buried. But since your uncle is gone, and I'm gone, I don't want you to be alone in the world. I didn't lie to you when I told you that your father was a stranger I'd met in a bar. I just didn't tell you the whole truth. He was a stranger, and we did meet in a bar one night. I was with my girlfriends, and he walked over to me with the most beautiful smile I'd ever seen. We left the bar together and went to a diner where we talked until two a.m. We started seeing each other after that night for a few months. I knew he was in a relationship with another woman, but I didn't care. He had stolen my heart in so many ways. He told me I was his soulmate and that he could never love another woman the way he loved me, and he was planning on breaking it off with the other woman. The best thing that had ever happened to me was finding out I was pregnant with you. The night I was to tell him about you, he had come over to tell me that we couldn't see each other anymore because the woman he was with was pregnant and she was carrying quadruplets. He said he needed to do the right thing, so he asked her to marry him. I was distraught and so angry. I'd felt like my heart had been ripped into a million tiny pieces, and I hated him for that. I begged him to stay with me. He told me he couldn't, and as soon as he was married, he was moving to California to start his own company. I figured if he could hurt the person he claimed so much to love, he would hurt you one day as well. So, I never told him I was pregnant. I'd kept tabs on him and his wife after they moved to California. Two months before you were born, she had her babies, and he had become the father of four boys. He was the reason I never married or was involved in a long-term relationship. I could never love anyone as I loved him.

Your father's name is Henry Kind. He lives in California and is the owner of Kind Design & Architecture. He's your blood, my *darling son, as are your four brothers. You don't need to do anything with this information, but I couldn't rest in peace until you knew the truth. You're not alone in the world, Shaun. As you're reading this, I'm sure anger and hate for me have consumed you. All I wanted to do was protect you, whether you believe me or not. Just know that I love you very much, and I will always watch over you.*

Love, your mother

She was right. I was angry at her for never telling me the truth. But I was more furious at the man who hurt and abandoned her.

After rereading the letter for what seemed like the hundredth time, I stared at the birth certificate that came with it. My actual birth certificate. The one where the name *Henry Alexander Kind* was listed in the box under "Full name of Father."

~

The following morning, I made a cup of coffee in my to-go mug and headed down to the car that was waiting by the curb. When I entered the building where Sterling Capital Corp. was, I took the elevator up to the twenty-first floor and headed straight to the conference room to meet with Bill Gaffey.

"Morning, Bill," I spoke as I stepped inside and closed the door.

"Morning, Shaun."

Setting my cup down on the conference room table, I unbuttoned my suitcoat and took the seat across from him.

"Well? What do you have for me?"

"Are you sure you're ready for this?"

"I've been ready ever since I first read that letter."

"Your father, Henry Kind, is now retired from Kind

Design & Architecture. He left the company in the hands of Sam and Stefan Kind, two of your brothers. Both boys oversee the entire company. Sam runs the architect division, and Stefan runs the building and construction."

"What about the other two?"

"All four boys are stockholders in the company and are on the board. Sebastian went the way of becoming a chef. He owns two 5-star Michelin restaurants. Four Kinds in Venice Beach and Emilia's in downtown Los Angeles. Your other brother, Simon, is a detective with LAPD. A well-respected detective." His brow raised. "Whom, by the way, is lying in a hospital bed recovering from a gunshot wound."

"Is he okay?"

"He's going to be."

"Tell me more about my father."

"Well, he's on his fifth marriage. After he married his current wife, Celeste, he handed the company over to his sons. Also, you should know that he and his wife are expecting a baby."

"Jesus Christ." I shook my head. "Are you serious?"

"Yes, Shaun. Very serious."

"And my four brothers?"

"Sam is married to a woman named Julia who is also pregnant. Stefan was a single father to a little girl named Lily until he met Alex. They have since married and have a son together named Henry."

"So, I have a niece and nephew, another on the way, and a sibling coming?"

"Yes. Sebastian lives with a woman named Emilia, and they have a dog named Ruby. As for Simon, he's single. The four of them, including your father, live on a stretch of the beach in Venice."

"They all live next to each other?" My brows furrowed.

"Yes. The house your father lives in originally belonged to

Sebastian's girlfriend, Emilia. She sold it to Henry when she moved into Sebastian's house."

"They're just one big happy family, aren't they?"

"So, it seems. What now?" Bill asked.

"Get me the city housing map. I want to look at it. Keep watching them and report back to me. I need some time to devise my plan before putting it into action."

~

One Month Later

I was sitting behind my desk when Bill walked into my office.

"What's up, Bill?"

"I found someone who may be of interest to you." He handed me a file folder.

Opening it, I stared at the picture of the beautiful woman inside.

"Who is this?"

"Her name is Jenni Benton, and she's Julia Kind's twin sister. She's single and extremely close with the entire Kind family. She was a fashion model who recently retired and is now seeking an investor for her fashion label."

"Interesting." I stared at her smiling eyes. "Does she live close to them?"

"She lives in downtown L.A. in an apartment in the Circa building."

"And you're sure she's single?" I glanced up at him.

"She's definitely single."

My phone rang, and when I looked over at it, I saw my realtor, Bella Marcus, was calling.

"Hey, Bella. I hope you have good news for me."

"I do, Shaun. The Bennett's have accepted your generous offer for their house."

"Excellent. When can we close?"

"Ten days. They're asking for you to give them at least ten days after closing to move out."

"That's fine."

"Great. I'll get all the paperwork ready and call you when they need to be signed."

"Thank you, Bella. I appreciate your hard work."

"You're welcome, Shaun. Let me know if you need anything else. Take care."

"What was that about?" Bill asked.

"I just purchased the house on the beach next to Simon Kind."

"I didn't realize it was for sale."

My lips formed a smirk. "It wasn't. But who would be stupid enough to turn down triple the value and an all-cash deal?"

"Smart. So, I take it you'll be heading to California soon?"

"Yes. Very soon."

"There's something else," he said.

"What?" I arched my brow.

"Your brother, Simon, and a woman named Grace Adams checked into the Mandarin yesterday."

"He's here in New York?"

"Yes."

"For how long?"

"Their Delta flight leaves tomorrow at noon."

"Interesting. Thanks, Bill. I appreciate everything you've done. I'll be in touch." I got up from my chair and extended my hand to him.

"You're welcome, Shaun. I hope things work out for you with this family."

"Oh, they will." I smirked. "They aren't going to know what hit them once I'm through."

I left my office and walked over to my personal assistant, Selena.

"Can I help you?" Her brow arched as she looked up from her computer.

"I need you to call Rob over at Delta and find out which seat Simon Kind is sitting in on the noon flight to L.A. tomorrow. Then, I need you to book me the seat across from him."

"And if someone is already sitting in that seat?"

"Tell Rob they need to be put somewhere else because they were double booked. Also, I need you to reserve me a room at the Mandarin right now. I don't care which room. And I need you to meet me there in a couple of hours. Bring a few dresses with you, and make sure one of them is black."

"What?" She shook her head.

"Just do what I say."

I walked away and heard her shout.

"Shaun, what is going on?"

"Do it, Selena!"

CHAPTER 2

*S*haun

After taking a seat in one of the chairs at a high-top table in the bar area, I pulled my phone from my pocket and sent Selena a text message.

"Black dress. Hurry up and get down here."

As I sipped on my drink, I watched my brother and his girlfriend Grace up at the bar. She was a tough cookie. That much I could tell. And so was he. I could tell by the look in his eyes when he walked over that he was ready to kill.

"I'm here." Selena walked over and took the seat closest to me.

"You look nice. Now, you're supposed to be my blind date, so act like we're getting to know each other."

"You know, Shaun, I don't think I get paid enough for this. I have a date with Nick tonight."

"I pay you well, and you know it." I smiled. "You can go on your date as soon as they leave. Tell Nick to meet you here, and the two of you can order room service on me and keep the room for the rest of the night."

"Really?" She grinned.

"Yes."

I watched as Simon and Grace stood up from their stools. Turning my attention back to Selena, I caught both of them staring my way out of the corner of my eye. And come tomorrow, we'd meet again.

The following day, I'd met them again on the plane to California. We talked for almost the entire duration of the flight. Simon told me how he'd gotten shot and how he and Grace had met. He mentioned his brothers in a few conversations, and from what I could tell, they were extremely close. I was careful with my words and didn't divulge too much information about myself. All Simon Kind knew was that my name was Shaun, that I worked in capital and investment, and I traveled to California on a business trip.

"Do you need a ride somewhere? We'd be more than happy to drop you off wherever you're headed."

"Thanks, Simon, but I have a car and driver waiting for me. It was great to see you two again. Thanks for making the flight a good one." I smiled.

"Take care, Shaun." He patted my back.

"You too."

When I entered the baggage claim area, my driver held up an iPad with my name across the screen.

"I'm Shaun Sterling." I walked over to him.

"Welcome to California, sir. I'm Bernard, and I will be driving you to the Ritz Carlton."

"Thank you, Bernard."

As soon as my luggage came around, I grabbed my guitar case while Bernard grabbed my two suitcases and took them out to the limousine parked at the curb.

"Welcome to the Ritz Carlton. May I help you?" the cute redhead behind the desk asked.

"Reservation for Sterling."

"Welcome, Mr. Sterling." She smiled. "We've been expecting you. Here is your keycard to the Ritz Carlton Suite. If there is anything you need or that we can do for you, just let us know."

"Is the car I reserved ready?"

"Yes. It's with our valet. I'll have the bellman bring up your luggage."

"Thank you." I smiled at her and headed towards the elevator.

When I stepped inside the suite on the twenty-fifth floor, I looked around at the 2,920 square foot space with the city view.

"Excuse me, Mr. Sterling. I have your luggage," the bellman spoke. "I'll just put them in the bedroom."

"Thank you."

I took off my suit coat and loosened my tie. Grabbing a hundred-dollar bill out of my wallet, I handed it to him when he placed my luggage.

"Thank you, Mr. Sterling. This is much appreciated." He grinned. "Enjoy your stay."

"You're welcome." I gave him a nod as he left my suite.

I walked over to the large table that sat ten and looked at the large fruit and nut basket that sat on it with a bottle of champagne chilling in a bucket. Going over to the mini-bar, I grabbed the bottle of scotch I requested, poured myself a drink, walked over to the large window, and stared out at the city that was now my home for—well, I wasn't sure how long I would be here.

Throwing back my drink, I grabbed my guitar case, took out my guitar, and sat down on the oversized gray curvature couch. I strummed a few chords first and got lost in the song I played.

When I was four years old, my mother took me to the doctor for my extreme behavioral issues. She was convinced I was either bi-polar or just a plain old psychopath. But after long and many tests, it turned out I was brilliant with an IQ score of 150. The simple fact was that I was bored. Since she couldn't afford to send me to a private school for gifted children, I had to go to public school, which was too easy for me, leaving me bored and causing even more behavioral issues.

When I was eight years old, my mother bought me a guitar from a secondhand store to keep me busy while she left me alone and went out at night with men she never intended to get into relationships with. Men that made her moan at night and left before the sun rose the following morning.

When I was thirteen, my Uncle Ronin, my mother's older brother, walked into our lives. They had been estranged since I was two due to a stupid disagreement because both were so stubborn. At that time, I was smoking pot and got into all kinds of trouble in school, including fights with the other kids. I didn't take anything seriously because I was so angry all the time. Mad that I didn't have a father, angry that my mother worked a lot plus went out at night, and the fact that I had to take care of myself. She figured since I was an intelligent kid, I didn't need looking after. I often questioned why she even had me in the first place. And I'd often felt like I was nothing but a reminder of the guy she had a one-night stand with.

My Uncle Ronin wasn't the best person in the world. He was an asshole, arrogant, and quick-tempered. It was no wonder his wife divorced him, and he lost everything. He moved back to New York and in with us until he figured out what he would do. He started making investments in stocks with the bit of money he had. He introduced me to the world of investing, and when a couple of the investments went south, I helped him out by researching the market and telling him what to invest in. He started using my intelligence to make as much money as possible. The money he made he blew on cocaine and prostitutes. I made a lot of money, as well, and kept it hidden from my mother. After graduating at the top of my class from Yale, I opened the doors to Sterling Capital Corp. at the age of twenty-one with the help of some investors who trusted me after I walked into their office and told them exactly what to do to increase their investments.

I finished my song, set my guitar in its case, closed it up, and leaned it against the wall in the bedroom. I'd spent the next week getting to know Los Angeles, buying a large piece of land, and implementing my plan to get close to my newly found family.

CHAPTER 3

*J*enni
I was so excited when I'd finally found an investor for my fashion label. He was an older gentleman with a very business savvy sense. We'd met for dinner twice, and he genuinely seemed very impressed. He told me he'd invest in my company and give me everything I needed.

The night I went to his hotel room to sign the contract, he proceeded to tell me, not in a discreet way, that if he were to invest in my company, I would be obligated to thank him by sleeping with him every time he came to Los Angeles, which was at least three times a month. I refused, threw a glass of wine in his face, and told him to shove his investment up his ass. I was so humiliated that I didn't tell anyone what had happened. I'd already been through six rejections, and this was the straw that broke the camel's back. I was tired of men thinking I was just another pretty face that could be bought and used for their disgusting pleasure.

I'd spent a week hiding in my apartment even though I'd told

Julia and everyone else that I was going out of town. I wanted to wallow in self-pity alone, and I didn't want to be bothered. As I was sitting on the couch sketching, there was a knock at the door. I had ordered take-out, and when I went to open it, Simon stood there holding up the plastic bag with my food in it.

"What are you doing?" I asked with an arch in my brow.

"The question isn't what I'm doing. It's what are *you* doing?" He kissed my cheek and stepped inside.

"Did you quit your job as a detective and start up your own food delivery service?"

"Very funny." He set the bag on the kitchen counter. "It just so happened that Grace and I were leaving the restaurant when I overheard the Uber Eats guy say he was there for a pickup for Jenni Benton. Then I thought to myself, how is that possible since you're out of town." His eye narrowed at me. "So, I gave him a tip, took the food, and told him I'd deliver it to you myself."

"They aren't supposed to do that," I said as I narrowed my eye.

"He fought me at first until Grace pulled out her badge and said you were a suspect in a murder case we were investigating, and it was in his best interest to stay away from you and your place. He happily handed over your food." He grinned. "What's going on?"

"I just got back." I smiled as I pulled out my sandwich and fries from the bag.

"Really? Because I don't see your suitcases anywhere."

"They're in the bedroom." I knitted my brows.

"You're lying." A smirk crossed his face. "You know you can't lie to me. I'll ask you one last time, what is going on?"

"First, where is Grace?"

"I had to drop her off at the station. She needed to do something."

He walked over to where I stood in the kitchen and gripped my shoulders.

"What happened that you lied to us and told us you were out of town?"

"Remember that investor I told you about? The one I was meeting to sign the contracts?"

"Yeah." His brows furrowed.

"When I got to his hotel room, he held the papers in his hand and told me that if he was going to go through with the deal of investing in my fashion label, one of the terms of the agreement was that I would have to sleep with him every time he came to L.A. for business."

I watched as Simon inhaled a sharp breath.

"Where is that motherfucker?"

"He's gone. I threw a glass of wine in his face and told him to shove his investment up his ass."

"Come here." He wrapped his arms around me and pulled me into him. "I'm sorry, Jen."

"It's fine, Simon." I held back the tears that were starting to fill my eyes.

"The four of us already told you that we'd give you the money."

"And I appreciate it, but I am not taking money from you or your family."

"We're your family, Jen."

"Doesn't matter. Family, money, and business do not mix. I'll eventually find someone." I broke our embrace.

Opening the container, which contained my cherry chicken salad wrap, I held it up to Simon.

"Bite?"

"No, thanks." A tender smile crossed his lips. "Listen, I don't like what you did. You said you were out of town, but you were locked up here all week. Don't do it again. We're here for you, Jenni. I'm here for you."

"I know. I just wanted to be alone to gather my thoughts and figure out what was next. Maybe this is the universe's way of telling me that I'm not meant to start my label."

"Nonsense. You have amazing designs, and any woman would be happy to wear your clothing."

"Thanks, Simon. But you're only saying that because I'm your bestie."

"That isn't true. You know I always tell it like it is. If I thought for a moment you sucked, I would tell you." A smirk crossed his lips. "But I don't, and neither does anyone else. You know tonight is family dinner at Four Kinds, and you better come."

"I don't know," I whined.

"Think about it because we all want you there." He kissed my forehead. "I have to go and pick up Grace. I'll see you tonight." He pointed at me as he walked away.

"We'll see!" I shouted as he walked out the door.

On the one hand, I wanted to go because I missed seeing everyone, but on the second hand—hell, enough with the self-pity. I needed to go out and have some fun tonight.

When I stepped through the door at Four Kinds, I saw the four brothers standing at the bar talking. As I approached them, I let out a gasp at the incredibly sexy man they were talking to.

"Jenni." Sam smiled as he placed his hand on my upper back and kissed my cheek. "I didn't know you were back."

"We'll talk about that later." I smiled as I looked over at Simon, who gave me a wink.

"Well," I flirtatiously smiled, "Hello, there. I'm Jenni." I extended my hand.

"Shaun." The corners of his mouth curved upward as he placed his hand in mine.

17

CHAPTER 4

*S*haun

I stared into her beautiful blue eyes as I shook her hand. I didn't expect all my brothers to be here tonight, let alone her. She was even more gorgeous and sexy in person than in her pictures. Five-foot-eight, long brown hair with subtle waves throughout, beautiful lips with a smile that made her eyes light up, high cheekbones, and a killer body. One that I wanted to explore badly. There was no way in hell this woman was single.

"So, how do you know these fine gentlemen?" she asked.

"Grace and I met Shaun in New York," Simon spoke.

"Yeah." I smiled. "I thought for a minute Grace was the woman I was meeting for a blind date."

"Oh, so you're single?" She grinned.

"I am." I placed my hand in my pants pocket. "Then it just so happened that Simon and Grace were on the same flight as I was. I came here for dinner because it was rated as one of the top restaurants and imagine my surprise when I saw him heading towards me. I had no idea that his brother owned the place."

"It's an excellent restaurant and the food is superb. You'll love it."

"I'm sure I will."

"We didn't know you were coming. We already ate, but I'll have Marco fix you a plate," Sebastian said.

"Or you can join me for dinner." I smiled at her.

She bit down on her bottom lip. "I'd love to."

"Excuse me, Mr. Sterling?" A woman walked over. "Your table is ready."

"Simon, my friend, it was good to see you again. Sam, Stefan, Sebastian, it was a pleasure to meet you." I shook their hands again.

"It was nice to meet you too," they all spoke.

"Watch out for that one," Simon gave me a wink and a smile as he patted my back. "Enjoy your dinner."

"Thanks, and I will." I chuckled.

We were seated at a table for two outside with a perfect view of the ocean. Between the warm temperature, light wind, and the sounds of the waves hitting the shoreline, it was an ideal evening to have dinner with a beautiful woman.

"Hi, Jenni." Our waitress walked over.

"Hi, Marcia. This is Shaun. Shaun, Marcia."

"It's nice to meet you, and welcome to Four Kinds. What can I get you two to drink?"

"I'll have a glass of Chardonnay," Jenni spoke.

"And I'll have a single malt scotch, 17 years."

"Excellent. I'll go grab those for you while you look over the menu."

"Is there anything you suggest?" I asked as I stared at her from across the table.

"The pecan-crusted whitefish is to die for."

"Sounds delicious. I'll take your word for it." My lips formed a smirk.

Our waitress returned, set our drinks down in front of us, and took our dinner order.

"So, tell me the story about how you thought Grace was your blind date."

"The woman I was meeting said she had long dark hair and she'd be wearing a black dress. When I walked into the bar at the hotel, I saw a woman with long dark hair wearing a black dress, so I assumed it was her. I honestly thought Simon was going to kill me when he walked up. I had to explain myself quickly."

She let out a laugh. "I bet you did."

"How do you know them?"

"Julia, who is Sam's wife, is my twin sister."

"Wow. Really?"

"Yeah. They're such a great family. We're all really close."

"I'd like to meet your sister sometime."

"You can meet her right now because here she comes." She grinned.

~

*J*enni

Julia walked over and placed her hand on my shoulder.

"Hey. Welcome back." She narrowed her eye.

"We'll talk later. Julia, I'd like you to meet Shaun. Shaun, my twin sister, Julia."

"It's a pleasure to meet you, Julia." He smiled as he extended his hand.

"It's nice to meet you, Shaun. Simon was just telling us about you."

"All good, I hope."

"Yes. All good."

"When are you due?"

"A couple more weeks." She smiled as she placed her hand on her overly large belly.

"Julia is having twin girls," Jenni spoke.

"Wow. Congratulations."

"Thank you. I'm so ready for them to be born right now."

"I bet."

"Anyway, it was nice to meet you, Shaun. Jenni, we're going to have a little chat later."

"Yes, ma'am."

I couldn't help but laugh.

"What was that all about?" I asked.

"Nothing. I told all of them I was going out of town, but I wasn't, and I stayed in my apartment all week."

"Why?" My brows furrowed.

"It's a long and boring story. Tell me, what brings you to California?"

"Business."

"What kind of business are you in?"

"I'm the CEO of Sterling Capital Corp. in New York."

I knew it. I could tell just by how he carried himself that he was a corporate man. Six foot three, striking blue eyes, brown hair that was stylish with tapered sides and a longer top, a masculine jawline with a neatly trimmed five o'clock shadow, and a muscular body I wanted to see more of.

"Nice. How long are you here for?" I asked.

"I'm thinking of opening an office here in L.A, so I'm sticking around for a while."

"Really?" Excitement flowed through me.

"Yes. I have a project I'm planning, and I need to get with some architectural firms."

"Seriously?"

"Yeah." He chuckled. "Know of any good ones in the area?"

"Actually, Sam and Stefan own Kind Design & Architecture. They're one of the best."

"No shit. I had no idea. I'll have to set up a meeting with them."

"Definitely. You won't be sorry."

"Again, I'll take your word for it." The corners of his mouth curved upward.

Marcia walked over and set our plates down in front of us.

"Is there anything else I can get you?"

"I'll have another glass of Chardonnay." I smiled.

My phone pinged with a text message from Julia in our girl's group chat.

"Bathroom, now!"

"Will you excuse me for a moment, Shaun? I need to use the ladies' room."

"Of course."

I grabbed my purse and when I opened the bathroom door, Julia, Alex, Emilia, and Grace, were all in there.

"I see you met, Shaun." A grin crossed Grace's face.

"We've been spying on you." Emilia smiled.

"He's a handsome guy." Alex smirked.

"I saw the way you were looking at him. You're going to sleep with him, aren't you?" Julia asked.

"With any luck. Look at him, wouldn't you?"

"I would." Emilia nodded.

"Me too," Alex said.

"I'd totally hit that." Grace smiled. "Plus, he's only here on business. You might as well have some fun with him while you can."

CHAPTER 5

*S*haun

As I sat there eating my dinner and waiting for Jenni to return from the bathroom, I glanced over and saw Sebastian talking with a couple a few tables over. As I stared at my brother, I greatly resembled all four of them. It was the first thing I noticed when I saw them standing together. People always told my mother I didn't really look like her, and I must have gotten my father's genes. She would politely smile and change the conversation.

"Sorry, it took me so long." Jenni smiled as she took her seat. "The girls were in the bathroom too."

"That's okay. By the way, you were right about this white-fish. It's excellent. Probably the best I've ever had."

"Good. I'm happy you like it." Her eyes lit up.

"So, Jenni—" I gestured for her to tell me her last name.

"Benton." The corners of her mouth curved upward.

"So, Jenni Benton, what is it that you do?"

"Well," she picked up her glass of wine, "I used to be a fashion model."

"Used to be?"

"I recently retired from the modeling business to start my fashion label."

"First, I'm not surprised you were a model. You are simply stunning. Second, are you a designer?"

"I've always wanted to be. I was all set to go to Parsons in New York after high school."

"What happened?"

"One day, I was with my mom at the mall the summer I graduated from high school. There was a fashion shoot going on, and everyone was standing around watching. Suddenly, the model fainted in the middle of the shoot. It was a clusterfuck of madness. Anyway, this guy walks up to me and says, 'You. Have you ever modeled?' I told him no, and he said it didn't matter and asked me if I would fill in for the model. I laughed at him and told him no. He told me they would pay me twenty-five hundred dollars for a couple of hours of work. All I kept thinking was how that money would come in handy for New York. So, I agreed after my mom and I went over the contract. A couple of days later, the agency contacted me and asked me to come in. I did, and they made me an offer I couldn't refuse. The rest is history."

"Wow. Talk about being at the right place at the right time." I smiled. "Why did you quit?"

"I traveled a lot, and I was getting tired of it. Plus, I wanted to be home for Julia and Sam with the twins on the way. I'd been thinking a lot over the past year about wanting to start a fashion label of my own, so I just decided I'm going to do it."

"Good for you. Congratulations." I held up my glass to her.

"Thank you." A wide grin crossed her lips as she dinged her glass against mine. "Do you have any family in New York?" she asked.

"No. I don't. My uncle passed away last year, and my mother passed away three months ago."

"Oh. I'm so sorry. What about your dad?"

"I never knew him. According to my mother, he was a stranger she met in a bar and spent one night with."

"Been there. Done that."

"Me too." I chuckled. "Tell me about your boyfriend."

"What makes you think I have one?" She cocked her head.

"A gorgeous woman such as yourself can't be single."

"Thank you for the compliment, but I am. I'm one hundred percent perfectly single and flying solo."

I narrowed my eye at her. "How is that possible?"

"Because I tend to date nothing but losers."

"Ah, I see. Am I a loser?" I smirked.

"I haven't decided yet." The corners of her mouth curved upward. "Besides, is this a date?"

"It can be if you want it to be."

She sat across from me with a flirtatious smile perched on her lips. A beautiful, cock hardening smile.

"What about you? Why is a sexy man like yourself not taken? Or are you?" Her eye narrowed.

"No. I'm not taken. Relationships aren't my thing. It's complicated."

"I feel you, Shaun." She slowly shook her head. "I think dating a lot of different people is educational. You're always learning something from them and the experience."

"Touché, sweetheart." I held up my glass again, and she tapped hers against it with a smile.

We talked for a while more, and it was getting late.

"We should probably go. It's getting late," I said as I stood up from my chair.

Holding out my hand to her, she placed hers in mine as I helped her up.

"Thank you."

"You're very welcome. Can I walk you to your car?"

"I'd like that." She grinned.

I placed my hand on the small of her back as we walked out of the restaurant, and she unlocked the door with her key fob when we approached her car.

"Thanks for dinner, Shaun. I really needed that tonight," she spoke as her body leaned up against the side of her car.

Bringing the back of my hand up to her face, I softly stroked her cheek.

"You're welcome."

As I stared into her eyes, I leaned in and brushed my lips against hers. She accepted my kiss as our tongues met, and I held her face in my hands. Breaking our kiss, I tried to catch my breath as I gazed at her.

"You could always come back to my apartment," she softly spoke.

"Was this a date?" I asked.

"Yeah. It was a date. But I don't think you're a loser."

"Then I must politely decline."

Her brows furrowed. "Why?"

"Because I want a second date with you. I don't want one night, and then we don't see each other again. What are you doing tomorrow?"

"I don't have any plans."

"Good. Then I'll pick you up at your apartment at eleven o'clock."

"In the morning?" Her brow arched, and I chuckled.

"Yes. In the morning. I would like you to go furniture shopping with me."

"Furniture shopping?"

"I bought a house here, and it needs to be furnished. I strongly believe you have a good design sense, and I could use your help."

The corners of her mouth curved upward. "I do have a good design sense, and I'd love to go shopping with you."

"Good. Then I'm going to need your phone number." I pulled my phone from my pocket.

As she rattled it off, I keyed her number in my phone and then held it up.

"Smile."

"What?" She laughed.

"Just smile for the camera." I grinned.

She flashed a beautiful smile, and I snapped her picture. Then I set it as a photo under her contact information.

"Address?" I arched my brow.

She rattled it off, and I stored it in my phone.

"Thank you. Drive safely." I stroked her cheek.

"What about your number?" Her brow arched.

"You'll get it when I text you to say goodnight." My lips formed a smirk. "Have a good night, Jenni."

"You too, Shaun."

CHAPTER 6

*J*enni

I climbed in my car and let out a deep breath. Another deep breath. And another. Holy moly, the fire down below was scorching hot. As much as I appreciated him being a total gentleman, I was disappointed he wasn't coming back to my place. I'd already made up my mind the moment he placed his hand in mine when I introduced myself that I would sleep with him. Letting out a sigh, I drove home.

After starting the bath and pouring in some of my Champagne bubbly bath fizz, I pinned my hair up in a messy bun, grabbed a glass of wine, and climbed in. Taking in a deep breath, I sipped from my glass and closed my eyes. I couldn't shake the feeling of how different Shaun was from any other guy I'd been out with. Even though I barely knew him, there was something so familiar about him. Something comforting and warm.

Grabbing my phone, I sent a text message to the girls in our group chat.

"Facetime?"

"Definitely," Julia replied.

"Yes," Grace wrote.

"Yes," Emilia replied.

"Of course," Alex wrote.

Opening the Facetime app, I selected all their names.

"I can't believe you're calling us," Julia spoke.

"Why are you in the bathtub alone?" Grace asked.

"Did Shaun boy turn you down?" Simon grinned as his face appeared behind Grace.

"Very funny. For your information, he's a perfect gentleman. Unlike you four douchebags who would have sex within seconds of meeting someone."

"Glass houses, Jen. Glass houses." Simon smirked.

"Ignore him," Grace spoke. "What happened?"

"Yeah. I'm dying over here." Emilia smiled.

"We had a nice dinner, and then he walked me to my car. We kissed, and I asked him to come back to my place. He asked me if I considered our evening a date, and I told him yes. Then he said—" I paused.

"Spit it out, sis!"

"He said he had to politely decline because he didn't want one night, and then we don't see each other again, and he wants a second date."

"Oh my God. How sweet is that." Alex placed her hand over her heart.

"I knew there was something special about him when I first met him." Grace grinned.

"He's picking me up at eleven o'clock tomorrow morning, and I'm going furniture shopping with him." I took a sip of my wine.

Alex furrowed her brows. "Why furniture shopping?"

"He said he bought a house here."

"Wait. I thought he was just here on business," Grace spoke.

29

"That's all I know. I'll find out more tomorrow. I got lost in his dreamy blue eyes, so I didn't think to ask him to elaborate on why he bought a house here. Oh, wait. He did mention something about maybe opening an office here."

"You look like you're smitten." Julia's lips formed a smirk.

"I'm not sure what I am. But I can't wait to see him again tomorrow. Oh my God, he's Facetiming me. Talk to you girls tomorrow. Love you."

I immediately clicked over and accepted his Facetime call.

"Wow. Damn. Hello there." A sexy smile graced his face.

"Hi." I flirtatiously smiled.

"Nice bubbles. Maybe I should have come over."

"Don't worry. I have more. I see you're staying at the Ritz Carlton."

"I am." He turned his camera around and showed me the suite.

"Very nice."

"Maybe tomorrow you can see it in person." He slyly grinned.

"I'd like that."

"Anyway, I was going to text you goodnight, but I wanted to see your beautiful smile one last time before I head to bed. I had a good time tonight, and I look forward to seeing you tomorrow."

For the love of God, I was speechless.

"I did too."

"I'll let you get back to your bath because something is starting to happen that I can't seem to control. Goodnight, Jenni, and sweet dreams."

"Goodnight, Shaun. I'll see you in the morning."

"You definitely will." He gave me a wink before ending the call.

~

*S*haun
       I set my phone down and poured myself one last scotch before heading to bed. Jenni Benton certainly was some woman. I could tell just by the little time I'd spent with her that she was fierce, strong, and independent. When she'd asked me to go back to her place, it took every bit of strength I had to tell her no because I wanted nothing more than to throw her on the bed or up against a wall and fuck her. Just the thought made my dick throb. But I needed to be careful and play my cards right. I needed her to trust me, for she was my quickest way into my family.

Picking up my guitar, I sat on the edge of the bed and strummed a few chords. As I sat there and thought about Jenni in the bathtub, I knew why Simon told me to watch out for her. I got the feeling the two of them knew each other a little too well. Setting my guitar down, I stripped out of my clothes and climbed into bed. As I was scrolling through my emails, my phone rang, and Bill's name appeared.

"What's up, Bill?"

"I was just curious to see how things are going over there in L.A.?"

"So far, so good. I met Jenni Benton tonight."

"I thought you were waiting a while?"

"She just happened to come into the restaurant when I was there talking to my brothers."

"They don't suspect, do they?"

"No. Not at all."

"Be careful, Shaun. This whole plan could blow up in your face."

"Don't worry. I will be."

I ended the call, plugged my phone into the charger, and laid it on the nightstand. Placing my hands behind my head, I lay there and thought about my brothers and Jenni. With any luck, I'd see them tomorrow when I took Jenni to see my new house.

The following morning, I ordered room service, showered, and got ready to pick Jenni up. When she opened the door, her cheerful smile captivated me.

"Come in." She gestured.

"Thanks. Nice place." I looked around.

"Thank you. I have to grab my shoes and purse, and then we can go."

She headed down the hallway, and when I looked over at her dining room table, I noticed all her designs sitting on it. Walking over, I picked one up and studied it.

"You did all these?" I asked as she walked over.

"Yeah. What do you think?"

"I think they're great. You're very talented."

"Thank you. Are you ready?"

"Yeah." I smiled at her as I placed my hand on the small of her back.

We took the elevator down to the lobby, and the doorman grinned before we exited the building.

"Have a great day, Jenni."

"Thanks, Stuart. It won't be hard with this handsome man." She patted my chest.

"You might think differently after you've been furniture shopping with me." I gave her a smirk.

CHAPTER 7

*S*haun
    We crossed the street, and I opened the passenger side door for her.

"You're such a gentleman. Thank you." Her lips formed a grin as she climbed inside my car.

"I thought it would be a good idea to go to the house first to get an idea of the layout before shopping for furniture."

"You haven't seen it yet?" she asked.

"Only pictures online. So, we'll be seeing it together for the first time." I gave her a wink.

I punched the address into the GPS and pulled away from the curb.

"Wait. That's where your house is?" She pointed to the address on the screen.

"Yeah. Why?" I glanced over at her.

"That's Mr. and Mrs. Bennett's house. The house next to Simon's and his other brothers."

"What?" I acted like I was shocked. "You're kidding me, right?"

"No. I swear to God." Her eyes widened. "How did you find it?"

"My realtor back in New York found it for me. I told her I wanted a house on the beach not too far from L.A. I have a high-rise penthouse in Manhattan, and I wanted to escape the city life. So, she called me one day and told me that it would be going on the market, and she sent me the listing. I fell in love with it and immediately put in an offer."

"That is crazy!" Her eyes lit up.

We pulled into the driveway and climbed out of the car.

"That's Simon's house right there." She pointed. "And next to him is Stefan, Sam, Sebastian, and the boy's father, Henry, lives in the house next to Sebastian."

"What?" I cocked my head. "They all live on this stretch of the beach?"

"Yep." A beautiful grin crossed her lips. "And now you do too. Oh my God, you are going to love living here. And the best part is, you'll fit right in with them."

I smiled at her as I held out my arm.

"Shall we go see the inside?"

"I'd love to."

Pulling out my key, I inserted it into the lock and pushed open the door to the Cape Cod oasis. Stepping inside, we entered the foyer that was off the living room. Light gray walls with bright white trim encased the area with a fireplace, built-in bookshelves on each side, and sliding floor-to-ceiling glass doors that led to the beach.

"Wow. Just wow," Jenni said.

Off the living room was a gourmet kitchen made of light gray walls, white cabinets, and black Italian marble countertops.

"Ah, you have a costly built-in coffee/espresso machine." She grinned. "I hope you're a coffee lover."

"I am." The corners of my mouth curved upward.

On one of the kitchen walls was a nook with built-in seating. Walking up the L-shaped staircase, we stepped onto the second level and into the primary suite that featured a sitting area, fireplace, and private balcony with a stunning view of the ocean.

"This is amazing. I love how the previous owners painted all the walls a soft gray color throughout the house."

"So, do I. It's the same color as my penthouse in New York." I walked over to the doors that led to the balcony and stepped out.

I could see my brother's houses perfectly from up here.

We toured the rest of the upstairs, which housed two more bedrooms with private bathrooms. After heading back downstairs, Jenni pulled out what looked like a sketch pad from her oversized purse.

"What's that?" I asked.

"A sketch pad. I'm going to do a quick drawing of the area. That way, when we go to look for furniture, you'll know exactly what will fit."

"Brilliant idea, Miss Benton." I smirked.

"I'm surprised you didn't hire an interior decorator," she said as she walked around with her sketch pad.

"It's my space, and I want to personalize it myself. Besides, I had an interior decorator once and fired her within a week. She just left a sour taste in my mouth as far as decorators are concerned."

"Oh. Well, let's decide right now to agree to disagree." She tapped me on the chest with her pen.

I let out a chuckle. "Deal. But I have a feeling I'm going to trust your word."

As soon as she was finished with the living room, I opened the sliding door and stepped onto the patio. The one thing I didn't like was the large stone wall separating my view from Simon's house.

"This has to go." I pointed.

"Why? Don't you like privacy?"

"I do, but it feels claustrophobic to me. At my penthouse in New York, I have a two thousand square foot open terrace."

"Damn. I'd love to see your penthouse sometime."

The corners of my mouth curved upward as I glanced over at her. "I'm going to have to go back to New York here and there to check in on the office. You'll come with me."

Her face displayed a bashful smile. "Okay."

We stepped back inside the house and went out the front door so that I could lock up. As we were walking to the car, I heard Simon's voice.

"Jenni? Shaun?"

"Oh, hey!" Jenni waved.

He walked over and shook my hand.

"Hey, man. What's going on here?"

"Howdy, neighbor." I smiled.

"You bought this house from the Bennett's?"

"I did."

"Isn't that crazy?" Jenni asked with a smile.

"I was flabbergasted when Jenni told me you and your brothers lived next door."

"I didn't know you were planning on staying in California?"

"Like I told Jenni, I'm thinking about opening an office here. As much as I love New York, the city can be draining. My mother passed away a few months ago, and besides my company, there isn't anything or anyone keeping me in the city. Plus, the weather is nicer here. After last year's brutal winter, I am more than ready to leave."

"I'm sorry to hear about your mom," he said.

"So am I." Jenni pouted as she placed her hand on my shoulder.

"Thank you. I appreciate it. By the way, gorgeous car." I pointed.

"Thanks, but it's Grace's car."

"Damn." I shook my head.

"Anyway, I have to run. Welcome to the beach, bro." He shook my hand again. "Listen, we're all getting together tonight at Sebastian's for a barbeque. We'd love for you to join us."

"No one told me about that?" Jenni's brows furrowed.

"That's because Sebastian just told me like five minutes ago."

Her phone dinged, and when she pulled it from her purse, she smiled.

"Let me guess. Sebastian?" Simon asked.

"Yes. Do you want to go?" Jenni glanced over at me. "I promise you'll have a really good time."

"I would love to go. Are you sure Sebastian won't mind?" I looked at Simon.

"Not at all. The more, the merrier." He patted my shoulder. "I'll see you two later." He kissed Jenni's cheek and walked away.

I couldn't help but narrow my eye when he did that. Why the hell was he kissing her cheek? Like I'd said, there was more going on with those two, and I was going to find out what it was.

We climbed into my car and drove to a high-end furniture store. When we stepped through the door, an older woman with short blonde hair walked over to us.

"Good afternoon. Is there anything I can help you find today?"

"I'm going to be spending an obscene amount of money,

so let us look around, and then I will let you know when we're ready."

"Very well." She grinned. "I'm Cheri." She extended her perfectly manicured hand.

"Shaun Sterling." I lightly shook it.

"It's nice to meet you, Mr. Sterling. Mrs. Sterling." She looked at Jenni and extended her hand.

"Oh, I'm not Mrs. Sterling. But don't tell her we were in here." Jenni gave her a wink.

"Umm—okay." Her brows knitted. "Can I get you two a glass of Champagne?"

"That would be lovely." Jenni grinned as she hooked her arm around mine. "Baby, do you want a glass?"

"Yes. That would be great." I looked at Cheri.

She gave us a nod with a light smile and walked away.

"Really, Jenni?" My lips formed a smirk as my one brow raised.

"She shouldn't have assumed. Let's start with the living room." She walked away, and I chuckled while shaking my head.

Cheri handed us a glass of champagne, and we spent the next two hours looking at furniture.

"I found the perfect throw pillows for that couch you like," Jenni said. "What do you think?"

"Navy blue?" I raised my brow. "I don't need pillows."

"What?" She cocked her head. "Yes, you do. Every sofa must-have throw pillows. Besides, they match that navy blue chair over there you're going to buy two of."

I turned my head and looked at the chair.

"I was already looking at that gray one." I pointed.

"Umm...no."

I looked at her with furrowed brows.

"Listen, Mr. Decorator. You can't have just gray, gray, gray. It would help if you had pops of color around, or your beautiful home will look boring. And, you know what they say?"

"No. Actually, I don't."

"Your home is a reflection of your personality. Do you want people to think you're boring?"

"Do *you* think I'm boring?" I asked with an arch in my brow.

"If you only have gray, gray, gray, everywhere, then yes. Cheri, tell him he needs the pillows and the navy-blue chairs."

"She does have a point."

"Fine. Add two of the chairs and the pillows."

"And this beautiful coffee table with the matching end tables?" Jenni grinned.

"Yes."

"Yay." She beamed with excitement. "It's going to look amazing. Just you wait and see."

After picking out a table for the breakfast nook, a dining room table and chairs set, a primary suite set, an additional bedroom set, some furniture for my office, bar stools for the kitchen island, some throw rugs, and outdoor furniture, it was time to check out.

"How soon can I expect delivery?" I asked Cheri.

"Next week."

"Not going to work for me. I need it delivered ASAP. You said everything is in stock."

"It is, but we do have other deliveries scheduled, Mr. Sterling."

I pulled my wallet from my pocket and took out five one-hundred-dollar bills.

"How soon can I get my furniture delivered, Cheri?" I set the money on the counter and slid it across to her.

"Ah, let me check again." She glanced at her computer. "Will Monday work?"

"Monday is perfect. Thank you."

"You're welcome. I have you scheduled between the hours of ten a.m. and two p.m. The delivery team will call you when they're about fifteen minutes away."

"I'll be anxiously awaiting." I smiled.

CHAPTER 8

*J*enni

"That wasn't so bad." I grinned as we walked out of the store.

Taking my sunglasses out of my purse, I slipped them on as we walked to Shaun's car. Walking over to the passenger's side, he opened the door for me.

"Are you hungry?"

"Starving." I climbed inside.

"How about lunch at the Ritz Carlton?" He climbed in and fastened his seatbelt.

"If I'm not mistaken, the restaurants there aren't open for lunch."

"What?" He glanced over at me in his Ray-Bans. "Seriously?"

"Seriously."

"Well, we can always order room service. You said you wanted to see my suite in person." The corners of his mouth curved upward into a sexy smile that made my legs tighten.

"Sounds good to me. I love room service." My lips formed a smirk.

He pulled up to the valet at the hotel, and we both climbed out of the car. We took the elevator up, and when we reached his suite, he swiped his keycard and opened the door.

"After you." His hand gestured.

"Thank you." I stepped inside and took in the luxury of the living area. "Oh, look." I walked over to the dining table and admired the silver platter of chocolate-covered strawberries.

"Open up." He smiled as he picked up a strawberry and brought it up to my mouth.

Taking a bite, I closed my eyes for a moment and savored the decadent and sweet taste.

"Oh my God, that is so good." I opened my eyes and stared at Shaun, who stood there with a smile on his face.

Bringing his hand up, his thumb lightly wiped the corner of my mouth.

"You have some chocolate right here."

I swallowed hard as his thumb gently swept over my lips.

"You are so beautiful, Miss Benton," he spoke in a mere whisper. "Would you mind if I kissed you?"

"No. Not at all." My knees weakened as my heart pounded.

Placing his hand on the side of my face, he leaned in and brought his lips to mine, giving me a soft and subtle kiss. I inhaled the smell of him. Warm, woodsy, and exotic. A scent that left a burning desire deep inside.

He pulled away, and our eyes locked on each other's for a moment before he kissed me again. A passionate kiss where our tongues intertwined, and our lips danced as if they couldn't get enough of each other. His hands roamed up and down the sides of my body before bringing his fingers up and pushing down the thin straps of my sundress. His tongue slid down my neck and traced my bare shoulder as his hand unzipped my dress from the back, and it fell to the ground. Picking me up, he buried his face in my cleavage, carried me to the bedroom, and laid me down on the bed.

As he hovered over me, his eyes stared into mine as his hand traveled down my torso and down the front of my black lace panties. I gasped as his fingers circled my clit in a soft motion that drove me insane. The wetness poured from me as the corners of his mouth curved upward.

"I can tell how much you're enjoying this."

"You have no idea." I fumbled with the buttons on his shirt.

"How about this?" One finger dipped inside me, and I let out a gasp.

"Yes. God, yes," I moaned as I pushed his shirt off his broad shoulders, exposing his muscular chest.

He dipped another finger inside, and I took him in. Throwing my head back, moans escaped my lips as he explored me. His mouth trailed across my neck as the orgasmic feeling erupted inside me. I wanted to scream with delight at what this man was doing to me. The sensation riddled my body with pleasure, and heaven opened its gates as I orgasmed.

"Beautiful," he whispered.

~

*S*haun
My cock was trying to bust out of my pants. I had never been so turned on as I was at that moment. Removing my fingers from her, I reached around, unclasped her bra, and tossed it over the side of the bed. My eyes left hers and diverted to the supple breasts with perfect hardened peaks that stared back at me. Bringing my mouth down, I wrapped my lips around her nipples and gently sucked each

one for a few moments before sliding my tongue down her taut torso. Gripping the sides of her panties, I took them down as my mouth slowly devoured her wet and swollen area. The area I couldn't wait to shove my hard cock into. Her hands tangled through my hair as I lapped up the pleasure that emerged from her. The sweet taste I'd craved since the moment I saw her.

Standing up, I pulled a condom from my wallet and took down my pants. The corners of her mouth curved upward into a sexy smile as her eyes stared at my cock. Sitting up, she scooted herself to the edge of the bed and wrapped her plump lips around me while gripping my shaft. Gratifying moans escaped me as I brought my hands to her head and held it. I wasn't expecting her to do this, which made it more exciting.

"Your mouth feels so good wrapped around me," I moaned as she continued sucking me off. "You need to stop, baby." I lifted her head. "I'm going to come within seconds, and I want to save it for when I'm inside you."

She smiled as she lay flat on her back. Tearing the package open, I slipped the condom over my cock and climbed on top of her, smashing my mouth against hers. Bringing my hand down, I felt to make sure she was ready for me because I didn't want to hurt her. The moment I thrust inside her, she wrapped her legs tightly around my waist and pushed me in deeper. I let out a moan, for the feeling was indescribable. Beads of sweat formed on my forehead as my heart pounded from my chest. Sitting back, I pulled her up against me as I thrust my hips, and our lips tangled. We stayed in that position for a few moments before I pulled out, rolled on my back, and brought her naked body on top of mine. My hands groped her luscious breasts, and my thumbs stroked her peaks as she rode me, and her body gave way to an orgasm. An orgasm that had my cock in its grip, causing me to explode inside her.

She leaned down and buried her face in the side of my neck as we both tried to calm our heavy breathing. Once we did, she climbed off me and rolled on her back. As satisfied as I was, I couldn't wait to be buried inside her again.

CHAPTER 9

*J*enni

He wrapped his arm around me and pulled me into his chest. All my happy hormones were sticking around as my body tried to calm down. It still trembled, and I couldn't escape the feeling that rose inside me.

"I hope I didn't disappoint you," he spoke.

"Absolutely not." I softly stroked his chest. "I hope you enjoyed it as much as I did."

"I can guarantee you that I enjoyed it more."

I smiled. "Not possible."

He let out a chuckle as his arm tightened around me.

"We never did place our order for lunch, and I'm starving," he said.

"Me too."

He reached over and grabbed the room service menu. Sitting up, I held the sheet over me as we viewed it together.

"I think I'm going to get the turkey avocado wrap," he said.

"That sounds good. I'll have that as well."

"Regular French fries or sweet potato fries?" he asked.

"Sweet potato."

He picked up the phone on the nightstand and placed the room service order.

My eyes diverted to the corner of the room, where I saw a black guitar case leaning up against the wall.

"Do you play the guitar?"

"I do." A sexy smile formed on his lips.

"Are you any good?" I smirked.

"I would hope so. I've been playing since I was a kid."

"Will you play something for me?"

"Right now?"

"Yes." I grinned.

"I need to use the bathroom first, and then I'll play something for you." He leaned over and kissed my lips before climbing out of bed.

I watched as he walked his hot and sexy naked body to the bathroom and let out a breath. Grabbing my panties from the floor, I slipped them on along with my bra and dress. When he emerged from the bathroom, he slipped his clothes back on and grabbed his guitar case. Following him to the living area, he set his case on the table, pulled out his guitar, and took it over to the sofa.

"What do you want to hear?" he asked as I sat down next to him.

"Anything."

"Okay. This is one of my favorite songs."

He slowly strummed a few chords first and then began strumming and singing *Don't Look Back in Anger* by Oasis. His eyes stayed locked on mine through the entire song, and I felt as if I was melting away. His sexy and raspy voice gripped me as the smile never left my face. When he sang the last word and strummed the final chord, I brought my hands up to my mouth for a moment and then started clapping.

"Wow. That was incredible. Oh my God, your voice is amazing. Did you take singing lessons as a kid?"

"No." He chuckled as a bashful smile crossed his mouth. "But thank you."

"How did you learn to sing like that?"

"I don't know. I just sing."

"Man," I shook my head. Sam, Simon, Sebastian, and Stefan, have some exceptional competition."

"What do you mean?" His brows furrowed.

"All four of them sing and play the guitar. They'll be doing it tonight. So, you better bring your guitar, and you can join in."

"Nah. I don't think so." He looked down in embarrassment.

There was a knock at the door, and Shaun got up and opened it.

"Your lunch, Mr. Sterling." A man pushed a cart into the room. "Where would you like it set up? At the table?"

"Yes. Please."

He went into the bedroom, walked out, and handed the man a fifty-dollar bill.

"Thank you, sir."

"You're welcome." He smiled at him.

"That was a very generous tip you gave." I smirked as I took a seat at the table.

"They work hard and deserve it. I can afford it, so I pass it on."

He poured us each a glass of wine.

I was in awe of this man already. Between his sweet nature, sex, and his generosity, my heart already fell head over heels for him. I needed to get to know him better, so I'd hoped he wouldn't mind all the questions I was about to ask him.

"Did you grow up in New York?" I picked up my turkey wrap and took a bite.

"I did. Born and raised. Tell me about this label brand of yours."

"Well," I picked up my glass, "there's not much to tell. Besides the designs and a few clothing manufacturers I've been in touch with, that's about it so far."

"Why is that? Are you not motivated to go any further?"

"Yes, I'm motivated." I knitted my brows at him. "It's just—"

"Have you spoken to investors yet?"

"I have. And I thought I snagged one until the asshole told me the only way he would invest would be that I had to agree to sleep with him when he was in town. He put that into the contract."

"What was his name?" His eye narrowed.

"Frederick Mason. The disgusting pig."

"Sounds about right." He sighed.

"Do you know him?"

"Yeah, I know him. And I'm not surprised he told you that. He's as slimy as they come. He did you a favor by telling you that. You would never have done well with him."

"Well, he was the last investor, and he was the reason I hid in my apartment for a week and told my family and friends I was out of town."

"Come on, Jenni. Seriously?"

"Yes, Shaun. That was the final straw. I'm a very strong and independent woman, and I can take a lot before I reach my breaking point. But I just kept feeling so rejected with every one of them, except for Frederick. He gave me hope, and then I told him to shove his investment up his ass."

Shaun let out a chuckle as he picked up his glass.

"Do you want to know my take on it?"

"Sure." I shoved a sweet potato fry in my mouth.

"They weren't the right investors for you and your brand. But I know someone who is."

"Who?"

"Me."

I couldn't help but laugh.

"Why are you laughing?"

"You want to invest in my company? Why? Because I had sex with you?"

"No. I'd already made that decision before we had sex when I picked you up this morning and saw your designs. I knew right then you have a special talent. I know you're going to make it in the fashion business, and I want to help you do that. You do realize that this is my job, right? This is what I do. Sterling Capital Corp. can be—what's the name of your brand?"

"Simply Jenni."

The corners of his mouth curved upward.

"Sterling Capital Corp. can be the seed money for Simply Jenni."

"I don't know, Shaun."

"Okay. Let me ask you this. Do you have a business plan already made up?"

"Yes. It's the first thing I did."

"Good. Then you'll give it to me tonight when I drive you home after Sebastian's. I'll take a look at it, give you my thoughts, and we'll go from there. Deal?"

"Fine. Deal." I smiled.

CHAPTER 10

*S*haun

After lunch, Jenni and I went shopping for all the home essentials I needed and took them to the house. Since everything else was back at my penthouse in New York, I was starting over. But I did pack some clothes and a few other personal things before I left, and the delivery truck with some additional stuff was scheduled to arrive on Monday.

"I can't believe you bought this expensive ass Vita-Mix," she said as she grabbed the box from the back of the car. "What's wrong with a regular blender?"

"I happen to make green smoothies every morning. Have you ever made one in a regular cheap-ass blender?"

"Yes. I make smoothies all the time—in my cheap ass blender."

"Wait until you make one in the Vita-Mix." I winked. "Your life will be forever changed, Miss Benton."

"We'll see about that." She flashed me a smirk. "I'll go take these towels and washcloths upstairs.

I was taking the new dishes out of the box in the kitchen when I heard a voice from behind.

"Hi."

Turning around, I saw a child with long blonde hair staring at me.

"Hello there. Where did you come from?" I furrowed my brows.

"Two houses down. I'm Lily. You must be our new neighbor."

Lily, my niece. Stefan's daughter.

"It's nice to meet you, Lily. I'm Shaun." I extended my hand.

"It's nice to meet you, Shaun. Welcome to the beach." She placed her small hand in mine.

"Thank you. Did you just walk in?"

"Yeah. Your sliding door is open." She pointed.

"So, it is."

"Lily?" Jenni spoke as she walked into the kitchen.

"Aunt Jenni!" She ran and hugged her. "What are you doing here?"

"I'm helping Shaun move some things in. What are you doing here?"

"I just wanted to introduce myself. It's the neighborly thing to do. I didn't know you two knew each other."

"Shaun is my friend." Jenni smiled. "In fact, he's coming with me to Uncle Sebastian's tonight."

"I won't be there," she said.

"Where are you going?"

"I'm spending the night at Maddie's house. Tomorrow is her birthday, and her parents are taking us to the Santa Monica Pier and Pacific Park."

"That sounds like fun."

"There you are." Stefan walked in, holding a baby. "Mom

is looking for you. You better head home and leave Mr. Shaun alone."

"It's okay, Stefan. She just wanted to welcome me to the beach." I smiled.

"Bye, Shaun. Bye, Aunt Jenni." She waved as she walked out.

"Sorry about that," Stefan spoke.

"No worries. She seems like a great kid. Who's this little guy?"

"This is my son, Henry."

"He looks just like you," I said.

"Yeah. That's what everybody says. I couldn't believe it when Simon told me you were the one who bought this house."

"Right? I was just as shocked when Jenni told me that all four of you and your father live on this stretch of the beach."

"Well, you're going to love it here, and we're the best neighbors in the world." He smirked. "I better get going. I'll see both of you over at Sebastian's."

"Bye, Stefan. Bye, little man." Jenni smiled as she kissed Henry's head.

"See you later." I gave him a wave. "Cute kid." I glanced over at Jenni.

"Yeah. He is. I am so excited about Sam and Julia's twin girls. I can't wait until they're born."

"I bet." I looked around at the mess that consumed the first level of my house. "Can you do me a favor and finish putting these dishes away. I need to get this mess cleaned up. It's driving me crazy."

"Of course. Wouldn't it be better to wait until we've put all this other stuff away?"

"No," I said as I started grabbing the empty bags and boxes.

Jenni laughed. "Don't tell me you're a clean freak."

"Is there something wrong with wanting things neat and organized?"

She turned and looked at me with furrowed brows.

"What?" I asked.

"You sounded just like Sam. For a second, I thought he was standing there."

I let out a chuckle.

"I'm serious. He's borderline OCD. Let me ask you something. Do you make your bed every day?"

"Uh, yeah. Right when I get up. Don't you?"

"Eventually." The corners of her mouth curved upward.

I walked over and gripped her hips.

"Can I give you a little piece of life advice?"

"Sure."

"Doing something as simple as making your bed first thing in the morning is tackling the first task of the day. It's a great way to start your day. Besides, an unmade bed looks messy, which leads to a cluttered mind. A clutter-free space leads to a clutter-free mind."

"Okay." She patted my chest, turned away, and continued putting the dishes away.

I still hadn't gotten around to asking her about Simon, and I didn't want to upset her, but I needed to know.

"Can I ask you a question?" I grabbed a garbage bag.

"Sure."

"What's up with you and Simon?"

"What do you mean?" She glanced over at me.

"The two of you seem very close."

"We are. Simon is my best guy friend. I tell him everything."

"Oh, okay. So, the two of you have never slept together? I just get this weird vibe that you have."

CHAPTER 11

*J*enni
Shit. Shit. Shit. I knew that would come back to bite me in the ass one day.

I inhaled a sharp breath. "We have slept together a couple of times."

He didn't need to know the exact number of times.

"But just as friends. Nothing else." I looked up at him.

"There weren't any romantic feelings between the two of you?" he asked.

"No. Not at all. He was just a friend with benefits, and then I cut it off because he meant more to me as a friend, and neither one of us wanted to compromise that."

"I see."

"If that's a problem for you, then I'll just go."

"Whoa." He put his hands up. "I was just asking, and it's not a problem."

He walked over to where I stood and wrapped his arms around me from behind.

"I think it's good that you put your friendship before sex. Ask me anything. Nothing is off-limits."

"Do you have a best 'girlfriend?'"

"No, and I don't want you to become one to me because I want to keep having sex with you." He kissed my cheek, and I smiled.

Turning around in his arms, I wrapped mine around his neck.

"You do?" I asked with a grin.

"Definitely. In fact," he placed his hands under my ass and lifted me while my legs wrapped securely around his waist, "I think I'm going to take you upstairs right now."

A happy grin crossed my lips. "There's no furniture, and the floors are too hard."

"Who said we need furniture or rugs? We have the countertop in the bathroom." The corners of his mouth curved upward as he carried me up the stairs. "That way, we can shut and lock the door. You never know who might just walk in the house."

"That just got me so wet."

"Good. Because I need to have a sweet taste."

He set me on the counter and shut the bathroom door. My heart was already racing, and the fluttering in my belly was in high gear. He lifted my dress, pulled off my panties, and tossed them on the floor. Getting down on his knees, he brought me to the edge and explored me with his mouth as I leaned back, and he brought me to the edge of no return. He stood up, pulled down his pants, slipped the condom over his beautiful hard cock, and placed one hand on the side of my face as his eyes stared into mine.

"Now you're ready for me."

As his lips meshed with mine, he thrust inside me as my nails dug into his back. I let out a gasp as the sensation gripped me. Soft moans escaped both our mouths as he thrust in and out. His hand groped my breast through the fabric of my dress as I lowered mine and firmly gripped his perfect ass, digging my nails into the flesh of his smooth skin. Another orgasm took over me as he held my hips, and with one last deep satisfying thrust, he buried himself deep inside me and let out a moan as he exploded. A smile fell upon his lips as he leaned in and whispered in my ear.

"Don't consider me a friend. Ever."

I threw back my head and let out a laugh as I placed one hand on his firm chest.

"I promise I won't."

"Good." He kissed my lips before pulling out of me and removing the condom.

"*D*on't forget to grab your guitar," I said as we were heading out the door.

"I have it."

We walked over to Sebastian's, and everyone was already there. Shaun stayed out on the patio with the guys while I went inside. As I walked into the kitchen, all four women stopped their conversation and stared at me.

"You're glowing," Julia said.

"I know that glow." Grace grinned.

"Me too." Emilia smiled.

"I know that glow all too well." Alex smirked.

"Spill it, sister." The corners of Julia's mouth curved upward.

"Spill what? I have no idea what you're talking about." I blushed.

"Liar!" Emilia said as she poured me a glass of wine.

"Fine. We had sex, twice. Once in his hotel room this afternoon and again about thirty minutes ago in his new house, up in the bathroom, and on the countertop."

"Yes!" Grace grinned as she held up her hand for a high-five. "Go, Jenni. Go, Jenni." She did a little dance.

"What's going on?" Simon asked as he walked inside and over to the refrigerator.

"Nothing," Grace said.

"Then what was with that little dance?"

"I can't dance with my girls?"

"Nobody else was dancing." He took a beer bottle from the fridge, flung the cap at her, and she caught it with one hand.

"We're having girl talk, Simon. No boys allowed."

"If you say so, baby." He kissed her before heading back outside.

"Judging by the smile on your face, I'd say it was everything you imagined?" Julia asked.

"More, sis. Way, way, way more." I grinned.

"The guys seem to like him already," Alex spoke as she looked out the sliding door at them. "You know what's kind of weird?"

"What?" I walked over to where she stood.

"Shaun kind of resembles the boys. Don't you think? More so, Sebastian."

"Yeah. he does," Grace said.

"I can see the resemblance," Emilia spoke.

"Anyway, when we were having lunch earlier in his hotel suite—"

"You mean after sex." Julia smirked.

"That too. He told me he wanted to invest in my company."

"Jenni, that's great!" Emilia said.

"I told him I had to think about it." I sighed.

"What? Why?" Alex's brows furrowed.

"Honestly, I don't know." I bit down on my lip.

CHAPTER 12

*S*haun

"Hey, Shaun." All four of them smiled and gave a wave when I stepped onto the patio.

"Hey. Thanks for the invite."

"No problem." Sebastian grinned as he patted my back. "Welcome to the beach, neighbor."

"Welcome to the beach." Sam grinned as he held up his beer bottle.

"Beer?" Stefan asked as he picked up a bottle from the table.

"Sure. Thanks." I set my guitar case down and took a seat next to Sebastian.

"You play?" Sam pointed to my case.

"I do, and Jenni insisted that I bring it. She told me that all four of you play as well."

"Yep. We do," Simon said.

"We wanted to start a band once when we were in our teens. We had big dreams." Stefan grinned.

"That's really cool. I just play to escape the craziness of life sometimes."

"I feel you, man." Sam shook his head. "We do too. Who taught you to play?"

"I taught myself. My mom bought me my first guitar when I was eight."

"You must have really been interested in music," Sebastian said.

"I wasn't. She bought it so I would keep busy while she went out at night. She did a good job of leaving me home alone a lot, and I liked to get into trouble. So, she figured learning the guitar would keep me out of trouble."

"Did it?" Stefan asked.

"Not really." I smiled. "But the more I learned to play, the more in love with music I became. I found that I would always turn to the guitar when I was having a bad day or if something didn't go my way. As I said, I play for the escape."

"That's how Emilia is with the piano."

"Really? Is she good?"

All four of them let out a chuckle.

"I'll have her play for you later," Sebastian spoke. "Her aunt was a pianist. Let's just say she inherited her musical talent."

"Wow. I can't wait to hear. By the way, Sam & Stefan. Jenni told me you two own and run an architectural firm."

"We do," Sam said.

"I have a large piece of waterfront property that I'm going to build luxury condos on, and I was looking for a company out here to design it for me."

"Excellent. Come to the office on Monday, and we'll have a meeting."

"Can we make it for Tuesday? Some of my things from New York are being delivered Monday, and I have furniture coming as well."

"Tuesday is good for me. You, Stefan?" Sam looked over at him.

"Yeah. Tuesday is fine. It'll have to be before noon, though," Stefan said.

"Will nine o'clock work?" I asked.

"We'll put you down on the schedule." Sam smiled.

"Hey, Simon, I just want to let you know that I'm going to have that wall on my patio removed."

"The one facing my house?" he asked.

"Yeah. It makes me feel a little claustrophobic."

"I don't blame you. I would have removed it too."

Suddenly, the sliding door opened, and I heard Emilia's voice.

"Look who came for a visit."

With the slight turn of my head, I saw him, my father, standing there holding an infant car seat in his hands.

"Dad. Celeste." All four of my brothers spoke as they got up from their seats and walked over to him.

"Hello, boys. We finally got to bring Nora home."

I sat there holding my beer and watched as hugs were exchanged and smiles were given while a feeling erupted inside me. Anger, hurt, resentment, and jealousy all rolled into one.

"Shaun, come over here," Simon said.

Would he see my mother in me? Would he know when he looked at me that I was his son?

Setting my beer down, I got up and walked over to where they all stood.

"Dad, I'd like you to meet Shaun. He bought the house next door to me. Shaun, this is our father, Henry Kind."

For the first time in thirty-three years, I stared into the eyes of my father and saw the same eyes staring back at me.

"Welcome to the beach, Shaun. It's nice to meet you." The corners of his mouth curved upward as he held out his hand.

"It's nice to meet you as well."

"This is my wife, Celeste. And this darling little princess is our daughter, Nora."

"She's beautiful. Congratulations to you both."

My heart pounded out of my chest as I stood there. I'd replayed this moment in my head over and over the past three months when I found out about him.

"We better get Nora home. We just wanted to stop by so she could see her family."

"Sure, Dad." Sebastian patted his shoulder. "Thanks for stopping by."

"We'll have all of you over soon so you can get to know your sister better. Again, it was nice to meet you, Shaun. You'll love living on this stretch of the beach. There's nothing quite like it." He stared at me.

"I'm sure I will."

I turned around, went back to my seat, and threw the rest of my beer down the back of my throat.

"Your dad seems nice," I said as my brothers sat down.

"He can be." Stefan smirked.

"It must be kind of weird having a newborn sister."

"You have no idea." Simon shook his head. "How old are you?"

"Thirty-three."

"You're the same age as us," Sebastian spoke. "Imagine if your mom or dad had a baby right now."

"I couldn't imagine."

"Another beer?" Sam asked.

"Do you have anything a little stronger?" I asked.

"You bet." Sebastian grinned as he got up and went into the house.

"So, Shaun, do you surf at all?" Stefan asked.

"I do a little bit."

"Good. You can join us sometime. We usually surf in the mornings on the weekends."

"Sounds fun. I'll make sure I buy a surfboard."

"There's this great surf shop over on Ocean Front Walk. Tell Jimmy I sent you," Simon spoke. "He'll take good care of you."

"Yeah. That's the only place we get our boards and gear from," Sam said.

"I'll check it out. Thanks."

Sebastian walked out and set the glasses on the table.

"Will this do?" He grinned as he handed me the bottle to look at.

"Scotland, 25 years." I smiled.

"Bro, where did you get that? And why have you been holding out on us?" Stefan asked.

"I haven't been holding out. I just got it a few days ago."

"Isn't that like fifteen hundred a bottle?" Simon asked.

"It is, and I think it's the perfect scotch to welcome Shaun to the beach." He took it from me and then poured us each a glass.

CHAPTER 13

Shaun

"Damn." I slowly shook my head. "That is some great scotch."

"Right?" The corners of Sebastian's mouth curved upward.

"Is it music time yet?" Jenni grinned as she and the other girls stepped onto the patio.

In the distance, we could hear rumbles of thunder and flashes of lightning over the water.

"Is it supposed to storm?" Alex asked as she sat on Stefan's lap.

"Let's take a look." Simon pulled out his phone. "Judging by the radar, it's heading this way."

"We should be okay as long as the rain blows the other way," Sebastian spoke.

Suddenly, it started to downpour.

"It's not blowing the other way!" Sam said, and we all jumped up from our seats and went inside the house.

"I guess we'll play inside," Sebastian said as he grabbed his guitar.

"Won't we wake the baby?" I asked.

"He's fine. Once he's out, he's out. We set up his pack n play upstairs," Alex said.

I took a seat on the loveseat, and Jenni sat down next to me with a glass of wine.

"You first, Shaun," Simon said.

"Yeah, man. We want to see and hear what you can do." Stefan grinned.

"Are there any requests?"

"Something by your favorite band," Sebastian spoke.

"Okay. Here it goes." I strummed a single chord for a test sound then went straight into the song.

"Yes! I love Oasis." Stefan flashed a smile.

I strummed the chords, and as I sang the lyrics to *Wonderwall* by Oasis, everyone sat there and stared at me with a shocked expression across their faces. Glancing over at Jenni, I smiled as I sang to her, and the grin on her face widened. After I strummed the last chord, I let out a breath.

"Damn, Shaun. You nailed that perfectly." Sam smiled. "Wow."

"Shit, man. You have some serious pipes," Sebastian spoke.

"I told you he was awesome." Jenni grinned before kissing my cheek.

I looked over at Simon, who sat there pointing at me.

"That was—that was—amazing." He stood up, walked over, and gave me a high five.

"Thanks, Simon."

We sat there playing our guitars and then listened to Emilia play the piano. The guys were right. She was amazing.

~

*W*e'd barely made it through the door of Jenni's apartment, and our clothes started to come off, leaving a trail to the bedroom. I held her arms over her head as I stared into her eyes while I slowly thrust in and out of her. The look on her face, the light moans that escaped her lips, and the warmth of being inside her filled me with pleasure—more pleasure than I'd ever felt in my life. I couldn't remember the last time I'd had sex three times in one day. Maybe that was because I never had. For me, it was always a case of wham-bam, thank you, ma'am, there's the door. But with Jenni, I wanted her any chance I could get, which concerned me.

"Are you okay?" I asked as she was snuggled against my body.

"I'm fine." She lifted her head and smiled at me. "Why?"

"Well, we did fuck three times today." My lips formed a smirk.

Her grin widened. "I know, and I thoroughly enjoyed every single time."

"Me too." My grip around her tightened. "It's late, and we should get some sleep."

"You're staying?" she asked.

"You don't want me to?"

"Of course, I do." She reached up and kissed my lips.

"In the morning, I'll look over your business plan, and we can discuss moving forward with your company."

"Shaun, you really don't—"

"Shush." I placed my finger over her lips. "Good night, Jenni."

"Good night, Shaun." She laid her head on my chest.

As I closed my eyes, thoughts of the evening infiltrated my mind. Spending time with my brothers was better than I expected it would be. I felt a connection with them that I hadn't planned on. As for my father, the anger still resided inside me. He may have been a good father to my brothers, but I grew up without one, and it was all his fault; his fault that my mother chose not to tell him about me.

When I opened my eyes the following morning, I expected to see Jenni lying there, but her side of the bed was empty. Rolling over, I grabbed my phone from the nightstand and looked at the time, which read nine a.m. I couldn't believe it, for I'd never slept in this late. Climbing out of bed, I pulled on my pants, made the bed, and walked to the kitchen, where I found her standing in front of the stove. Wrapping my arms around her from behind, I softly kissed her neck.

"Good morning."

"Good morning." She tilted her head to the side with a smile.

"I was very disappointed when I woke up and you weren't there."

"You were sleeping peacefully, and I was up, so I thought I'd make us some pancakes. You like pancakes, right? Cause who doesn't like pancakes?"

I let out a chuckle. "I like pancakes."

"Good. They're almost ready. Can I make you a cup of coffee?"

"It's okay. I'll make one myself. Where are the mugs?"

"In the cabinet above the Keurig."

Walking over to the cabinet, I took down a mug and placed it under the Keurig. Grabbing a k-cup, I popped it in and waited for the coffee to brew.

"When you're done with the pancakes, can you go get me your business plan?"

"It's on the table over there next to your plate." A bright smile crossed her face.

I gave her a wink, grabbed my coffee, and took it over to the table.

"Dig in," Jenni spoke as she set a plate of pancakes down in the center of the table with a bottle of syrup.

"Thanks." The corners of my mouth curved upward. "It's been a long time since someone has cooked breakfast for me. I'll return the favor once I get settled in the house."

"You cook?"

"I do. I'm not a professional like Sebastian, but I can cook."

Taking some pancakes, I put them on my plate, drizzled some syrup over the top, and began eating while I looked over her business plan.

"This is really good."

"The pancakes or my business plan?"

"Both." I smiled as I looked up at her. "Do you have a pen?"

"For what?" she asked.

"There are a couple of changes I'd like to make, and then you can let me know what you think."

She got up from her seat, grabbed a pen from the kitchen drawer, and handed it to me. After making the changes, I slid her business plan across the table to her. Picking it up, she looked at it and then up at me.

"Okay." She slowly nodded her head. "These changes are —are—"

My lips formed a smirk. "Go ahead. You can say it."

"They're acceptable changes."

"Good. Then you'll accept my offer to invest in your company/brand?"

She sat there and stared at me with her big beautiful blue eyes while biting down on her bottom lip.

"There should be absolutely no hesitation about this decision." I picked up my coffee and brought it up to my lips.

"I'm afraid."

"Afraid of what?" My brows furrowed.

"Mixing business with pleasure."

"Why?"

"Because it's a dangerous and poisonous cocktail and one that shouldn't be consumed."

"Ah, I see."

Picking up my phone, I opened my playlist and put on *Don't Wait Too Long* by Solomon Burke.

"What are you doing?" The corners of her mouth curved upward.

Standing up, I held out my hand to her and helped her up from her chair.

"Dancing with you." I wrapped one arm around her waist.

She let out a laugh. "Why?"

"Why not? Is it wrong that I want to dance with a beautiful woman?"

"So early in the morning?" She grinned.

"I didn't know there was a rule that states you can't dance in the morning." I smiled.

CHAPTER 14

*J*enni

There was nothing sexier than dancing with a half-naked man—especially a man like Shaun Sterling.

"Are you trying to charm your way into my company?" I gave him a smirk.

"Is it working?"

"Maybe."

As we swayed back and forth to the music, his blue eyes stared into mine.

"Listen to me. When I see a good opportunity, I act on it. How do you think I became so rich? I'm a very smart man, Jenni, and you need to trust me. But, if you don't feel comfortable having me as an investor, I can find someone else for you."

"No. I accept your offer." I smiled as he twirled me and pulled me into him.

"Excellent. I'll have my lawyer draw up the contracts, and you can move forward." His soft lips brushed against mine as he swooped me up in his arms. "Shall we go celebrate?"

"Definitely."

He carried me into the bedroom. When I looked over, I noticed the bed was already made.

"You made my bed?"

"Yes." The corners of his mouth curved upward.

"It's just going to get messed up."

"No, it won't. I'm bringing you in the shower with me." He gave me a sexy wink.

～

"I have to go and do some work back at the hotel," Shaun said as he slipped on his shirt.

"It's Sunday."

"I know, but there are many things that require my attention no matter what day it is." He gripped my hips. "And if you recall, I didn't get anything done yesterday." His lips met mine. "I'll be in touch later."

"Okay."

I walked him to the door, and his lips met mine once again before he walked out.

Letting out a sigh, I placed my hand over my heart and leaned up against the door. That man had me in such a tizzy, and I didn't know what to do. How could I feel such strong emotions for someone I barely knew?

Slipping on my shoes, I grabbed my keys and purse and headed over to Julia's house. I went around the back, and when I opened the sliding door, Sam and Julia were sitting at the table.

"I was hoping you were home."

Walking over to the Keurig, I grabbed a cup and popped in a k-cup.

"What's going on? Where's Shaun?" Julia asked.

"He had to go back to the hotel to do some work."

71

When the coffee finished brewing, I took my cup and sat down at the table with them.

"It's official. Sterling Capital is the new investor for Simply Jenni."

"That's amazing." Julia reached over and grabbed my hand.

"Congratulations, Jen." Sam smiled. "I think you made the right decision. I like Shaun."

"Yeah. So do I." I sighed as I looked down at my cup.

"What's wrong?" Julia asked. "Why did you say it like that?"

"Something is happening, sis."

"Like?" Sam arched his brow.

"I think I'm in love with him, and that's not possible because I barely know him. For fuck's sake, I just met him. This isn't me. You know what he did this morning?"

"What?" Julia asked.

"He made my bed."

"And what's wrong with that?" Sam asked.

"Nothing. He's a clean freak. I don't think he's as bad as you, though." I glanced over at Sam.

"Well, guess what? I like him even more." He grinned.

"Of course, you do, baby." Julia smirked at him.

"Maybe Shaun is meeting all of your expectations too quickly, and it's scaring you," Julia said. "Just take things slow, sis. As you said, you barely know him. I think right now, what you're experiencing is lust."

"Don't you have that perfect guy list?" Sam asked.

"Yeah."

"Get it out and start checking off the boxes." He smirked. "Once you do that, then you'll know for sure."

"Good idea. I think I will." I smiled. "Anyway, I need to run to the grocery store and then get home and finish a couple of designs I've been working on. Now that I have an investor, it's time to put my business plan into action." I kissed Julia's cheek and then Sam's. "I'll talk to you later."

CHAPTER 15

*S*haun
        "Thanks for meeting me on a Sunday, Tom." I shook his hand before we stepped inside the building.

"No problem, Shaun. Bella told me you need to get this secured quickly."

"I do." I looked around the space with my hands tucked tightly in my pants pockets. "My attorney has already looked over the sale of property contract, so all I need is a pen, and I can sign them."

He reached in his pocket and handed me a pen while he took out the contract from his briefcase.

"I've tabbed everywhere that needs your signature."

After I signed, Tom handed over the keys to the building.

"It was a pleasure doing business with you, Shaun. Hopefully, we can work together again soon."

"That's a possibility." I smiled as I shook his hand.

After Tom had left, my phone rang.

"Hey, Adam. Are you here?"

"Hey, Shaun. My plane just landed."

"Great. There's a car waiting to take you to the hotel. I'm

just wrapping up some business now, and I'll meet you over there."

"Okay, man. I'll see you soon."

I ended the call and placed my phone back in my pocket. Walking up the stairs to the second level, I looked around. After I had locked up, I headed back to the hotel. Just as I pulled up to the valet, I saw Adam getting out of the car that had brought him from the airport.

"Hello, my friend." I walked over and gave him a light hug.

"It feels like forever since I saw you last," he said.

"It's been a couple of weeks. Get yourself checked in and we'll go up to my suite and have a drink."

After Adam checked in, we headed up to my suite. Grabbing the bottle of scotch from the bar, I poured him a glass and handed it to him.

"Nice view up here," he said as he stared out the window.

"It is nice."

"So, what's going on with you and Miss Benton? Did she agree to let you invest?"

"In fact, she did. I was just over at the building I bought for her design studio."

"And your brothers?"

"They're nice people. I was at my brother Sebastian's house last night. Apparently, they all get together on the weekends."

"And?"

"I had a good time. I met my niece and nephew, and I also met my newborn sister, Nora."

"You saw your father?" His brow arched.

"I shook his hand." I brought the glass up to my lips. "You should have seen him. All proud of his daughter and acting like he was such a great dad. I wanted to punch him right in the face."

"And nobody suspects anything?"

"No. As far as they're all concerned, I'm just the guy who bought the house next to them."

"What about Jenni Benton?"

"She's already fallen head over heels for me."

"Poor girl." His lips formed a smirk.

"Yeah. I almost feel bad for her. If she only knew the truth."

"You better prepare yourself for when she finds out."

"I'm meeting with Sam and Stefan on Tuesday to go over the condo project."

"Have you figured a way yet into their company since its privately owned?"

"Not yet. I'll cross that bridge when the time comes." I set down my glass. "I'll have my home office set up tomorrow, and I'm going to hold a Zoom conference, so make sure everyone is available when you get back."

"I will. There's something I want to discuss with you."

"What is it?"

"Devlin Harris is threatening to pull his money out."

"Why now?" I sighed.

"He said Cooper Capital is offering a better deal, and if you don't do something, he's walking."

"Doesn't he know better than to threaten me?"

"You'd think. What do you want me to do?"

"Cooper Cap is slowly failing, and they're offering better deals to get investors on board. Let Devlin go. He'll regret it."

"Are you sure, Shaun?"

"One hundred percent. I have bigger plans for Cooper Cap." I held up my glass.

CHAPTER 16

*J*enni
     I thought I would have heard from Shaun by now, but I hadn't. It was seven o'clock, and I was starving. For some reason, I thought we were having dinner together. Grabbing my keys and my purse, I headed to Four Kinds. The restaurant was packed, so I went straight to the bar.

"Alex, what are you doing here? You don't work on Sundays?" I took a seat on the stool.

"Hey." She smiled. "Leslie went home sick, and Sebastian asked if I could cover for a couple of hours. Moscow Mule?"

"Lemon martini."

"I figured you were with Shaun tonight."

"I thought I would be too, but I haven't heard from him since he left my place this morning. He said he'd be in touch later. I guess his 'later' is different from mine." I sighed.

"You know men. They have no concept of time." A smirk crossed her face.

"Hey, Jen." Sebastian walked over and placed his hand on my back.

"Hi, Sebastian."

"Are you hungry?" he asked.

"Starving."

"Do you want the salmon with risotto and roasted asparagus?"

"Please." I smiled. "And that amazing bread and cherry butter?"

"I got you." He gave me a wink.

"Isn't Stefan pissed you're working tonight?" I asked Alex.

"He had a few choice words, but I promised to make it up to him when I got home, and his attitude quickly changed." She grinned. "I talked to Julia today, and she told me that Shaun is your new investor. Congratulations."

"Thanks. I'm excited to get my business off the ground and get my clothing into stores. I just hope I made the right decision."

"It's a business deal, Jen, with a little extra benefit on the side. I wouldn't worry about that. Shaun seems like a great guy, and he wouldn't invest in your company if he didn't believe in you or your designs. In fact, you can check that box on your perfect guy list." She gave me a wink.

"Funny you should mention that." I picked up my drink. "I took that list out today, and he's already checked many boxes. It's freaky."

"Not if he's the 'one' and you're meant to spend a lifetime together like Stefan and me."

Sebastian walked over and set my food down in front of me.

"Enjoy." He smiled. "By the way, where's Shaun?"

"Good question." I picked up my fork. "He's doing work stuff."

"Ah. Well, tell him I said hi when you see him."

After I finished my dinner, I headed home, put my hair up in a messy bun, took off my makeup, and put on my favorite nightshirt that was frayed and had a couple of holes in it. But I didn't care because it was soft, and we'd been through some tough times together. I picked up my sketch pad from the coffee table, sat down on the couch Indian style, and looked at my designs.

"Ugh. What was I thinking with this one?" I said aloud as I took my pencil and started redesigning the bottom half.

It was ten-thirty when my phone rang. Glancing over at it, my belly did a flip when I saw it was Shaun.

"Hello."

"Hello, beautiful."

"I'm sorry, but who is this?"

He let out a chuckle.

"You know who this is."

"Wait a second. Are you the guy who left my apartment this morning, never to be heard from again?"

"You're adorable. I left something at your door."

"What? When?"

"Don't worry about when. Just open it and see for yourself."

"It better be a box of chocolates from Edwart Chocolatier in Paris."

Getting up from the couch, I opened the door and jumped when I saw Shaun standing there with his luggage, guitar case, and a wide grin on his face.

"It's not a box of chocolates from Edwart Chocolatier, but I'm hoping I come pretty close."

I wanted to die because I looked like such a scrub.

"Oh my God. What are you doing here? You could have given me some notice. I look like I was just in a train wreck."

"You look gorgeous." He kissed my cheek and wheeled his suitcases inside. "I hope you don't mind if I spend the night. I already checked out of my suite."

"No. I don't mind. Why didn't you wait until tomorrow morning?" I asked as I shut and locked the door.

"You want the truth?"

"Yes."

"I missed you." The corners of his mouth curved upward.

"Shut up. No, you didn't." I bit down on my bottom lip as my bashful side emerged.

He walked over to where I stood and cupped my chin in his hand.

"Yes, I did." His lips met mine. "Plus, I'm hoping you'll come with me to the house tomorrow and help me decide where the furniture is going. I really need your expertise."

"I can do that." My lips formed a smirk.

"Thank you." His lips brushed against mine before his tongue parted my lips. "You taste like a lemon martini. Were you drinking alone?"

"Maybe I was with a guy." My brow arched.

"Lucky guy. Should I be jealous?" He wrapped his arms around me and pulled me into a tight embrace.

"Probably." I smirked as I broke our embrace.

"I should have called or even texted you earlier. I'm sorry. My CFO, Adam, flew in this morning. We had some business to go over, and I was with him all day."

"That's okay. I understand."

He stood there for a moment with a smirk across his lips, and one eye narrowed at me.

"Do you really?"

"It's doesn't matter." I smiled and sat down on the couch.

"Where were you tonight?" he asked as he sat down and hooked his arm around me.

"Four Kinds. Alex made me a couple of lemon martinis, and I ate dinner up at the bar while we talked."

"I'm sorry, Jen. I really should have called."

"You're fine, Mr. Sterling." I laid my head on his shoulder. "What do you think?" I held up my sketchpad.

"I like it, and I'd like to see you in it."

"As soon as my bundles of fabric come in that I ordered, I'll make it and try it on for you."

"Good. Then I can take it off you." He gave me a wink as I looked up at him. "Speaking of—I don't mean to offend you, but what's with this nightshirt? It looks like it's years old."

"It is. I've had it since high school. We've been through a lot together."

"Interesting. Like what?"

I let out a sigh as I sat up and faced him.

"The day I bought it, I found out my boyfriend of two years was cheating on me with multiple older women. It wasn't the first time he had cheated, and I was the stupid one for trusting him again. Anyway, after I came home that night sobbing and feeling like my life was over, I put it on and felt comforted. I can't explain it, and you probably think I'm weird."

"Maybe a little." He smirked.

"Shut up." I laughed as I slapped his chest. "It was new and soft and comforting. I don't know. I just can't seem to part with it."

"Okay. I sort of get that. But how about you part with it right now and climb up here."

CHAPTER 17

*S*haun

"The truck from New York arrived before the furniture did, so I had the guys set some of the boxes in a corner so they wouldn't be in the way when the furniture arrived."

"Sebastian is running over," Jenni said. "He's bringing some coffee beans so we can make some coffee."

"That's nice of him. All the boxes that say 'bedroom' go upstairs and in the first room on the left," I told the guys.

The sliding door opened, and Sebastian walked in.

"I bring java beans." He smiled.

"God, I love you," Jenni walked over and kissed his cheek as she took the bag of coffee from him.

"Hey, man." I smiled as I shook his hand. "Thanks. I'll buy a bag and send it over when I go to the store."

"Nah. Don't worry about it. That's what neighbors are for. Are you officially moving in?"

"Yep. This is my home now. I'm just waiting on the furniture to come."

"You piece of shit! How do you work this damn thing?" Jenni yelled.

Sebastian chuckled as he walked over and helped her.

"I have to run to the restaurant. Good luck, Shaun, and again, welcome to the beach."

"Thanks, Sebastian. I'll talk to you later."

"Are you okay now?" I arched my brow at Jenni.

"I'm great." She grinned as she held the white mug between her hands. "Want a cup?"

"Are you going to yell at the machine again?"

"No. I know how to work it now."

"Then, yes. I'd love a cup." I kissed her forehead. "Thank you."

"Do you want to watch so you'll know how to use it?" she asked.

"I already know."

"How?" Her brows furrowed.

"It's the same one I have in my penthouse."

"Oh my God! Why didn't you help me then?"

"I was going to, but Sebastian got to you first. I think the furniture guys are here." I walked away and opened the front door."

"Where do you want the TV?" one of the delivery men asked.

"It's getting hung on the wall above the fireplace."

"Okay. Again, where do you want me to put it?" he spoke with irritation.

"Above the fireplace." I raised my brows.

"Not our job. We don't hang TVs."

"I specifically asked my salesperson about it, and she said you would. I bought the kit."

"She was wrong, man. Sorry."

"Name your price?"

"Dude, I can't. Honestly, I don't know how to hang them.

I need you to sign this for me stating that we completed the delivery."

I grabbed the pen from his hand and signed the delivery sheet.

"Have a nice day."

"Yeah. You too."

I sighed as I ran my hand through my hair and stared at the box the TV was in.

"No worries. Stefan is coming over after work and hanging it for you."

"What?" I turned and looked at Jenni.

"I just texted him. He said he'd be more than happy to do it. He loves to do stuff like that."

"Thanks. I probably could have done it myself."

"Oh. Okay. I'll text him and tell him that you don't need him."

"No. No. If he likes to do it, then it's fine."

"That's what I thought." She scrunched her nose. "The furniture looks great in here. I'm in love with the navy-blue pillows and the chairs."

"I will admit, they do look good." I smiled at her.

"So, I was right?" Her brow arched.

"You were right. I really need to get my computers online, so I'm going to get my office set up."

"Okay. The sheets should be done drying. I'll go put them on and get your bed set up."

"You're going to make my bed?" I asked with surprise.

"Hilarious, Sterling." Her eyes narrowed, and I chuckled.

~

"*I* appreciate you helping me out," I spoke to Stefan as we removed the TV from the box.

"No problem. That's what friends do. Help each other out." He grinned.

It took him ten minutes to get the brackets up, and we were ready to hang the TV. I grabbed one end while he grabbed the other, and we securely set the TV in place.

"You're all set." The corners of his mouth curved upward.

I went to the refrigerator, pulled out a couple of beers, and handed him one.

"Thanks again." I held up my bottle to him.

"You're welcome." He smiled as he tapped his bottle against mine. "By the way, where's Jenni?"

"She ran over to Julia's."

"Jenni told us that your mom passed a few months ago. I'm sorry for your loss."

"Thanks. I appreciate it."

"Do you have any other family in New York?"

"No. It was just my mother, my uncle and me. He passed last year."

"What about your father?"

I brought the bottle up to my lips and took a sip of beer.

"I never knew my father."

"Oh. Gee, I'm sorry."

"Yeah. It is what it is. You're lucky yours lives right here. The four of you seem very close to him."

"Well, I wouldn't go that far. Don't get me wrong, we love our father, but it wasn't always easy with him."

"When did he and your mother divorce?"

"When we were five. His company and other women were more important at the time. I'm not sure if you know this, but Celeste is his fifth wife."

"Yeah. That's what Simon had said."

"He mustn't have been too bad of a father. The four of you seem like you've turned out great."

"Only because we had each other. I love my mother, but she had her own issues with men. So, between her and our father—"

"I feel you there." I shook my head.

I heard a tap on the sliding door and saw Simon standing there, so I waved him in.

"Hey. I went to your house, and Alex said you were over here. Hey, man." Simon walked over and fist-bumped me.

"I hung Shaun's TV for him," Stefan said.

"Looks great, bro." He patted Stefan's back.

"Do you want a beer?" I asked.

"Sure. Thanks."

I grabbed one from the refrigerator, and we went outside on the patio.

"You bought furniture for out here?" Simon asked as he took a seat.

"I plan on spending a lot of time out here. A view like this shouldn't be wasted."

"Exactly!" Stefan pointed at me.

"We're outside all the time, so feel free just to walk over whenever you want," Simon said.

"That goes for all of us," Stefan spoke. You're part of our circle now, and you're always welcome." He held up his beer bottle.

"Thanks, guys. That means a lot." Simon and I both tipped our bottles against his.

CHAPTER 18

$\mathcal{S}$haun

Jenni had spent the night at my new house, and we broke in the bed. We were up early because I needed to drive her home before meeting with Sam and Stefan. When I pulled up to the curb of her building, she leaned over and kissed me.

"Thanks for the ride."

"You're welcome. I'll call you later."

"Sure." A smirk crossed her lips.

Reaching over, I cupped her chin in my hand.

"I will call you later." The corners of my mouth curved upward.

"Okay. You better get going, or you're going to be late for your meeting."

I parked my car in the parking garage, walked inside the building, and took the elevator up to Kind Design & Architecture. When I stepped out of the elevator, I saw Sam standing at the front desk handing a folder to the receptionist.

"Good morning." He extended his hand. "Welcome to Kind Design & Architecture."

"Thanks." I shook his hand. "Great place you have here."

"Home away from home." He smirked. "Let's go to my office. Josh, can you let Stefan know that Shaun is here. Have a seat." He gestured as he took the seat behind his desk.

"Morning." Stefan grinned as he walked in and shook my hand.

"Morning."

"Coffee?" Sam asked.

"That would be great."

"Josh, three coffees, please," he shouted from his desk.

"So, where is your property located?" Sam asked.

"Pacific Palisades."

"Nice." Stefan smiled.

"I purchased two large lots overlooking the ocean. I need you to design the entire building and the grounds. I have the plot specs right here." I reached into my leather bag and pulled it out.

"Great. Let's take it over to the table and have a look."

Josh walked in with our coffees and set them on the table.

"Thank you, Josh," Sam said. "How many floors?"

"Six at the minimum. I want the design to be a modern coastal concept with an open floor plan."

"Number of bedrooms?" Stefan asked.

"One to three. I won't lie. After Jenni told me about your company, I did some extensive research and found Kind Design & Architecture is one of the best."

"And I won't lie. We are." Sam smirked.

"When are you looking to start?" Stefan asked.

"As soon as possible."

"Stefan and I need to go to the property, look around, and take some pictures. I can have a rough concept draft for you in a couple of weeks."

"That's fine. I need to head back to New York for a while for business."

"Is Jenni going with you?" Sam asked.

"No. She doesn't even know I'm going yet. I'm telling her today. Between getting her business off the ground and the impending arrival of your children, she doesn't have the time to come with me."

After we finished our meeting and all three of us exchanged phone numbers, I drove my car back to the rental shop and caught a cab to the dealership where I purchased a brand-new Audi R8 Spyder in the color Mythos Black and pulled up to Jenni's apartment building. Pulling my phone from my pocket, I dialed her number.

"Hey. What a surprise. I didn't expect to hear from you so soon."

"I told you I would call. What are you doing?"

"Looking over the fabric that was just delivered."

"I need you to put on your shoes, grab your purse, and meet me outside."

"For?"

"There's something I want to show you, and somewhere I want to take you."

"Okay. I'll be right down."

I sat in my car with my Ray-bans on and waited for her. The look on her face was priceless when she stepped outside her building and saw the car.

"What the—" A bright smile crossed her face.

"Get in." I grinned.

"Is this another rental?" She climbed inside.

"Nope. I just bought it."

"You bought this? Seriously?"

"I did. Do you like it?"

"I love it! It's so beautiful. Plus, convertibles are my favorite. Where are you taking me?"

"You'll see." A smirk formed on my lips.

I pulled around to the back of the building where the parking lot was. Climbing out of the car, I walked around, opened Jenni's door, and held out my hand.

"Thank you. What is this place?"

I led her to the door, unlocked it with my key, and motioned for her to go in first.

"Why do you have a key?" Her brows furrowed.

"I bought the building."

"For?"

"Welcome to your new office/design studio. This is where the magic of Simply Jenni is going to happen."

She placed her hand over her mouth in shock as she stared at me.

"You bought this for me?"

"Of course. You can't work out of your apartment. You need a real office, real space, and staff. Come on," I held out my hand to her, "I'll show you around."

"I can't believe this, Shaun."

"Do you like it?"

"I love it." She threw her arms around me. "Thank you."

"You're welcome." I brushed my lips against hers. "Let's go upstairs. I guess you could call this the break room. As you can see, it has a large refrigerator, a sink, and quite a bit of counter space. All you need is a couple of tables and chairs and maybe a couch along that wall."

"This is amazing."

I grabbed her hand and led her down the open hallway a few feet.

"And one of these will be your office. Take your pick. There's something I need to tell you," I said as we were walking down the stairs.

"What is it?"

"I need to head back to New York in the morning for a while."

"How long?"

"I don't know. A week, maybe two. I wish you could go with me, but you need to stay here with your sister, and you need to get this place up and running."

"I'm going to miss you." She pouted.

"You're going to be so busy that you won't have time to miss me." The corners of my mouth curved upward as I swept my thumb across her lips.

Her phone rang, and when she pulled it from her purse, she told me Alex was calling.

"Hey, Alex. What?" She exclaimed. "I'm on my way."

"What's wrong?" I asked.

"Julia is in labor. Alex is driving her to the hospital. I have to get there."

"Of course. Let's go."

CHAPTER 19

Jenni

We arrived at the hospital and went straight to the Labor and Delivery floor.

"Can I help you?" a nurse sitting behind the desk asked.

"My sister, Julia Kind, is in labor. Which room is she in?"

"Jenni," I heard Sam speak.

Turning around, I hugged him.

"How is she?"

"In a lot of pain. She's asking for you. Hey, Shaun. I didn't really think today would be the day."

Shaun placed his hand on Sam's shoulder. "Breathe, Sam. It's all going to be okay."

"I'm trying. We're waiting for the doctor to get here. I'll take you to Julia."

"I'll go wait in the waiting room," Shaun said as he grabbed hold of my hand and gave it a gentle squeeze.

"Okay. I'll see you in a while."

I followed Sam down the hallway and into Julia's room. The moment she saw me, she held out her hand as tears filled her eyes.

"Hey, you." I walked over, grabbed her hand, and kissed her forehead.

"Thank God, Alex was home," she said before letting out a gut-wrenching scream.

"It's okay, baby. Breathe. It'll be over soon," Sam said as he held her hand.

"I wasn't supposed to go into labor. That's why I scheduled the damn c-section!"

"You know things don't always go as planned. My two little nieces can't wait anymore to meet their mom and dad." I smiled.

"It hurts so bad."

Dr. Kota walked in and examined Julia as she squeezed both my and Sam's hands.

"One of the girls is breeched. Let's get her prepped for a c-section," he told the nurse. "Sam, you can go with the nurse, and she'll have you change into a pair of scrubs."

"You can do this." I leaned over and smiled at her as I placed my hand on her forehead. "I love you, sis."

"I love you too."

"Did you call Mom and Dad?" I asked Sam.

"Yes. They're going to try and get a flight back today."

"They better. I warned them not to travel so close to Julia's due date." I shook my head.

I went to the waiting room where Sam's entire family was waiting.

"Any news?" Henry asked.

"They're prepping her for a c-section right now."

I walked over to where Shaun was sitting and took the seat next to him.

"You don't have to wait here. I'll call you later."

"No, it's okay. I want to wait." He grabbed hold of my hand.

Sam's mom walked in and gave each of her sons a hug.

"Who's that?" Shaun asked.

"That's Barb, the boy's mother."

~

Shaun

I sat there and stared at her. The woman Henry chose over my mother. She walked over and hugged Jenni.

"Barb, I'd like you to meet Shaun Sterling. He's from New York and just moved into the house next to Simon's."

I extended my hand. "It's nice to meet you, Barb."

She placed her hand in mine and stared at me for a moment.

"It's nice to meet you as well, Shaun. What brings you to California?"

"Business," I replied.

"Shaun is a major investor in Simply Jenni."

"That's wonderful news. Congratulations, Jenni."

"Thank you." She grinned.

Something was off with that woman. I could feel it.

"I'm going to look for the restroom. I'll be right back," I spoke to Jenni.

"Okay."

I left the waiting room and found the restroom down the hall and around the corner. When I was finished and opened the door, I saw Barb standing there.

"Can I speak with you for a moment?" she asked.

"Um, sure."

"Has he figured it out yet?"

"Excuse me?" My brows furrowed.

"Don't play dumb with me. I know who you are. You have his eyes and the eyes of my four sons. I know one of Henry's children when I see them."

"I'm sorry, but I don't know what you're talking about."

"I think you do." She pursed her lips. "Henry may not know about you, but I do. I knew your mother was pregnant the same time I was."

I swallowed hard as I looked at her.

"Does anyone know?" she asked.

"No." I slowly shook my head. "How do you?"

"Your mother followed me one day into a coffee shop and told me everything about her and Henry. She was hoping that if I knew what a cheating bastard the man I was about to marry was, I'd leave him. But I wasn't about to do that with four babies on the way. Maybe if I weren't pregnant, I would have felt differently. I felt sorry for her until she told me she knew Henry and I were in a relationship but still carried on with him."

"Why didn't you tell him about me?"

"Because I was afraid if he knew, he'd run back to her, and I couldn't have that. I had four boys to raise, and I wasn't about to do that alone. I never forgot our conversation, and I married a man I knew cheated on me and was the father of another child. I knew in the back of my mind he would always be a cheater. I mean, look at the man. He's on his fifth marriage. Not because his previous wives passed or anything, but because he can't keep his dick in his pants for one woman. And you mark my words. He'll cheat on Celeste. Men like him don't change. Now I don't know exactly what you're doing here, but if you disrupt my son's lives in any way—"

"You'll what, Barb?" I arched my brow at her.

"Hey, there you are." Jenni walked over to us. "What's going on?"

"I just ran into Barb, and she was asking me about my company."

"Yes. Curtis and I are looking to invest, and I was just asking Shaun what my best options would be."

"Oh. Well, he's your man." Jenni grinned as she placed her arm around mine.

"It was nice talking to you, Barb," I spoke as we walked away and went back to the waiting room.

"Hey, man." Simon walked over. "Jenni told me about her design studio. She's really excited."

"Good. She needs a proper place to design and work. When my realtor found the building, I knew it was perfect for her."

"She told me you're leaving for New York tomorrow."

"Yeah. I need to get back to my office there and catch up on some things. I won't be gone long. In fact, would you mind keeping an eye on the house for me?"

"Not at all." He pulled out his phone. "It just dawned on me that we never exchanged phone numbers. Give me your number, and then I'll send you a text, so you'll have mine."

I rattled off my number as he keyed it into his phone."

"Sam!" I heard Jenni exclaim, and Simon and I both turned around.

He wiped his tears of joy as we all gathered around him.

"The girls are perfect, and Julia is doing well. Lena weighs six pounds four ounces, and Lorelei weighs six pounds three ounces. They're both healthy and amazing." His eyes filled with tears.

"Aw, you both did decide on Lena and Lorelei," Jenni said as she hugged him.

"The second we saw them, we knew. We just knew."

After everyone took their turns congratulating him, I extended my hand.

"Congratulations, Sam. I'm really happy for you and Julia."

"Thank you, Shaun. I appreciate it. As soon as you get back from New York, we're having you over for dinner."

"Sounds good." I smiled at him.

I stared at my father, who stood talking to Sebastian while Barb stared at me from across the room. I was uncomfortable, so I decided to leave.

"I need to make a few phone calls and take care of some business. You call me when you're ready to leave, and I'll pick you up."

"That's okay. I'm going to be here for a while. I'll catch a Lyft home, pack an overnight night bag, and meet you at your house later." A flirtatious smile crossed her lips.

"I was hoping you were coming over and spending the night." I brushed my lips against hers.

I said goodbye to everyone and took the elevator down to the lobby. As I was walking out of the hospital, I heard my name.

"Shaun?"

When I turned around, I saw Barb behind me. Letting out a sigh, I stopped.

"What do you want, Barb?"

"I know you're angry at him. I would be too. Hell, I still am after all these years. But my boys have nothing to do with this. They're happy in their lives, and they are not to know anything about you or their father."

"I'm their brother!" I shouted. "They have a right to know they have another sibling."

"Not at the expense that it will cause turmoil and disdain in their lives."

I stood there and slowly shook my head at her.

"Wait a second. This isn't about their lives. It's about yours and what they'll think and do to you when they find out you knew all along. Cause mark my words, lady, I will tell them."

"Don't you dare threaten me," she spat through gritted teeth.

"I'm not threatening you. I'm making you a promise." I stared at her for a moment before walking away and climbing into my car.

CHAPTER 20

*J*enni

After everyone visited and left, I stayed behind. I wasn't ready to leave my sister yet.

"They are absolutely gorgeous." I smiled as I stared at Julia and Sam as they each held their daughters. "I can't tell whom they look like. I think they're a combination of both you and Sam."

"Both of them definitely have Sam's nose." Julia smiled.

"And your beautiful lips," Sam said.

"Where's Shaun?" Julia asked.

"He had to go and make some business calls. He's leaving tomorrow to head back to New York."

"For how long?"

"A week or two. He's not really sure yet." I pouted.

"That's not too long. I'm sure you'll survive." She smirked. "Mom and Dad will be here first thing tomorrow morning. They're coming straight from the airport. They're so upset they weren't here."

"Well, it's their own fault. I'm going to go and let you rest. Plus, you haven't even been alone with Sam yet since the girls came into the world. I'll text you later to check up on you." I leaned over and kissed Julia's forehead.

"Are you going over to Shaun's house tonight?" she asked.

"Of course. I need to get one last fuck in before he leaves." I smirked as I gave her a wink.

Sam inhaled a sharp breath and slowly shook his head.

"You love it, and you know it." I kissed his cheek before I walked out of the room.

I went home, packed an overnight bag, and freshened myself up. I wouldn't lie and say I wouldn't miss Shaun because I would. The thought of him not being around for a week or two made my heart hurt, and that was something I didn't experience with the men I dated.

"Hello there, beautiful." Shaun smiled when he opened the door.

"Hi." I dropped my bag and wrapped my arms around him.

"You know you don't have to knock."

"I wasn't sure." I broke our embrace. "It smells like pasta sauce in here."

"That's because I'm cooking dinner for us." He kissed my lips, then grabbed my bag and took it upstairs.

Walking over to the kitchen, I took the lid off the pot on the stove and inhaled the aroma of the sauce cooking.

"It smells delicious. Homemade or jar?" I arched my brow as he walked into the kitchen.

"I'm insulted you even asked that. It's homemade." He picked up the wooden spoon from the counter and stirred it.

I grabbed the bottle of wine from the refrigerator and poured some into a glass.

"And where did you learn to make homemade sauce?"

"I taught myself. I did a lot of cooking when I was a kid. It was either I learned or ate macaroni and cheese every night because my mom didn't cook anything that didn't come from a box."

I didn't know what to say to that, so I just gave him a sympathetic smile.

"It's okay. Cooking is a skill every man should know. If she had cooked gourmet meals every night, I most likely never would have bothered to learn, and I'd be cooking you kraft mac n cheese right now." The corners of his mouth curved upward.

I shrugged. "I like Kraft Macaroni and Cheese."

The sliding door opened, and Sebastian walked in.

"I bring bread and butter." He grinned. "Wow. Your sauce smells great, Shaun."

"Thanks, Sebastian."

"Do you mind?" he asked as he removed the lid from the pot.

"Not at all. Go ahead." Shaun reached in the drawer and handed him a spoon.

"Wow. Yeah." He nodded his head. "This is really good. It only needs one thing."

"What?"

Sebastian leaned over and whispered in Shaun's ear.

"Really?"

"Yep. Trust me."

I stood there and narrowed my eyes at them.

"Don't give me that look," Sebastian said. "You know I have secret ingredients."

Shaun chuckled and patted Sebastian's back.

"Thank you again for bringing over the bread and butter. How much do I owe you?"

Sebastian put his hand up. "Nothing, man. It's on the restaurant."

"I can't let that happen. How much?"

"Nothing. I have to run. I'll talk to you both later."

"I can't believe he wouldn't let me pay for that," Shaun spoke.

"I can. He never does. Did you stop by the restaurant?"

"I did, and the bread was still baking, so he said he'll bring it home and drop it off to me. I know how much you love it, and I figured it would be good with dinner."

I wrapped my arms around him. "Thank you."

"You're welcome." He kissed the top of my head. "We better get dinner on the table before the noodles overcook."

He prepped the pasta while I cut the bread and took it over to the table. When we sat down, he took something out of his pocket and slid his hand across the table.

The corners of my mouth curved upward. "What are you doing?"

He lifted his hand, and I looked down at the shiny key sitting there.

"I figured you could use this if you wanted to come over while I'm gone. I'll also give you the alarm code. It might be easier for you since you'll be spending a lot of time at Julia's, and your studio is only seven minutes from here. I asked Simon to keep an eye on the house while I'm gone as well."

"Are you sure you want me to have this?"

"Of course. Why wouldn't I?" His brows furrowed.

"It's a big step." I gave him a smirk. "It almost makes me feel like we're seriously dating."

He picked up his glass and brought it up to his lips. "Are we?" His brow arched.

"You tell me."

"I can tell you this. I don't want you sleeping with anyone else while I'm gone."

"Same goes for you."

"Deal." He gave me a wink as he extended his hand across the table.

I reached my hand across and placed it in his. "Deal."

~

Several moans escaped my lips as he thrust in and out of me from behind, and my fingers gripped the sheets as an orgasm tore through me. I would miss this while he was gone, and I didn't want to think about tomorrow morning. I just wanted to enjoy the moment now and stay lost in him.

He slowed his pace and buried himself deep inside me as he came while his hands gripped my hips as if he was holding on for dear life. When he pulled out, I rolled on my back and wrapped my arms around his neck. He slowly lowered his body on mine and buried his face into the side of my neck. The warmth of his breath soothed me as my arms around him tightened. It was at that moment that I knew for sure I was head over heels in love with this man.

He lifted himself off, but not before kissing my lips. Rolling on his back, he held out his arm, and I snuggled into his muscular body.

"Are you okay?" he asked. "You're not as talkative as you usually are?"

I picked my head up from his chest and looked at him.

"Are you saying I talk too much?"

He chuckled. "No. But you're being quiet. Is something wrong?"

"Maybe you just wore me out, and I'm tired."

"That's a shame. I was going to have you climb on top for another round since this is our last time for a while."

"Oh. Well, I'm not that tired." I grinned as I climbed on top of him and smashed my mouth into his.

CHAPTER 21

*S*haun

The moment I stepped off the plane, I had my driver take me to the office.

"Do me a favor and drop my bag off at my penthouse," I told him as I climbed out of the car.

"Will do, Mr. Sterling."

I grabbed my briefcase and shut the door. When the elevators opened to Sterling Capital, everyone looked up from their workstations and welcomed me back.

"Thanks, everyone. I appreciate it." I gave a nod.

Walking up the stairs to my office, Selena got up from her desk and followed me inside.

"Welcome back, boss. How is California treating you?"

"It's good, Selena. How are things here?"

"Not bad. Adam is a good boss." She smirked.

"Not as good as I am, though, right?" I arched my brow.

"Well, he doesn't have me go on pretend blind dates."

"One time. That was one time. Anyway, where is Adam?"

"He's on his way in from a meeting across town."

"Welcome back." Adam grinned as he held up his hand for a high-five.

"Thank you, my friend. Selena, that'll be all."

She walked out of my office and shut the door.

"So, what's going on?" Adam asked as he sat down in the chair across from my desk. "How's your newfound family?"

"I have a little bit of a problem. Barb, the boy's mother, knows who I am."

Adam's brows furrowed. "How?"

"She said I have my father's eyes. Apparently, when my mother was pregnant, she tracked Barb down at a coffee shop and told her everything."

"Shit. She knew this whole time and never said anything to anyone?"

"I guess not. She's very adamant about me not telling my father or my brothers who I am."

"Because she's worried how it will affect her when they find out she knew, right?"

"Exactly." I leaned back in my chair and placed my hands behind my head.

"Are you worried about her?"

"Not really. She has a lot to lose. She's a smart woman, and she wouldn't be that stupid. Tell the staff that we're having a meeting in about fifteen minutes and to be prepared."

"Will do, Shaun."

It was eight o'clock when I'd left the office and headed home. After picking up some Thai food, I poured a glass of scotch and sat down at the table. My phone, which was sitting next to me, pinged with a text message from Jenni.

"I haven't heard from you all day. Just making sure you made it back to New York safely."

"I did, and I've been swamped today. Don't forget I haven't been here for a while."

"*I haven't forgotten. I was just—forget it. I'm glad you made it there okay. I'll talk to you later.*"

She was pissed. I could tell by the tone of her message and the way she abruptly cut it off.

"*Don't be mad. I'm very busy. Now that I'm back here, I have a lot of fires to put out.*"

"*Yeah. I understand. Like I said, I'll talk to you later.*"

"*You have an attitude, Miss Benton.*"

"*Actually, I don't. I'm very busy too, but I took a moment to text you because I care whether or not you died in a plane crash, Mr. Sterling.*"

I let out a chuckle and shook my head.

"*I'm fine. Just busy.*"

"*So, you've said a hundred times already. And I won't bother you again for fear that I will take you away for two seconds from all the fires you have to put out.*"

I let out a sigh. This was the main reason why I never got involved in a relationship. I needed to rectify this situation, so I dialed her number. On the first ring, it went to voice-mail. She had rejected my call.

"*Why did you reject my call?*"

"*Because I'm busy. If I wanted to talk on the phone, I would have called you instead of texting. Good night, Shaun.*"

"*Good night? It's only five o'clock in California.*"

I waited for her to respond, but she didn't. Rolling my eyes, I set my phone down and ate my dinner. I didn't need to play the role of a doting boyfriend when I was in New York.

Four Days Later

*J*enni

Before heading to my studio, I stopped by Sam and Julia's to check on them and the babies. When I walked through the sliding door, both girls were screaming as Sam and Julia held them and walked around the kitchen.

"What is going on in here?"

"Enter at your own risk," Sam said.

"Here, let me take her." I walked over to Julia and took Lorelei from her.

"I have no idea why they are both screaming. They've been fed, changed, held, sung to." Julia's eyes filled with tears. "Not to mention that Sam is having anxiety about the mess. And we're both so tired."

"Grab my phone from my purse," I told her.

She handed me my phone, and I texted Stefan, Sebastian, and Simon.

"Whichever one of you is home right now, get your ass over to Sam and Julia's house."

Suddenly, all three of them stepped through the sliding door.

"Wow. I didn't expect all of you to be home."

"I was just about to leave for the office," Stefan said as he took Lena from Sam and quieted her down. "Aw, she just wanted her Uncle Stefan." He grinned.

Sam rolled his eyes and gripped the edge of the marble countertop.

"You and Julia are to go upstairs and take a nap while we keep your children quiet. Go on. You have about an hour."

"I love you so much." Julia hugged me.

"I know. I love you too."

They left the kitchen, and Sebastian and Simon stood there staring at me.

"What?" I asked.

"Can we go?"

"Sebastian can go. You're staying." I pointed at Simon.

"What the fuck, Jen? Why?"

"Because I need your advice. Stefan, hand Lena over to him. I know you have to get to the office since Sam is off."

"What's going on?" Simon asked as he held Lena.

"I'm furious at Shaun." I took a seat at the table as I held Lorelei in my arms.

"How can you be? He's not even here."

"The day he left for New York, he didn't even bother to call or text me that he arrived safely. When I sent him a text message at eight o'clock that night his time, he gave me a real attitude."

"What did he say?"

"He said he was busy and had a lot of fires to put out, and I should know that because he hadn't been there in a while."

"Well, he does have a point. Listen, you know how text messages can come across. Do you think you're overreacting?"

"No." I frowned. "But he can't take two seconds to call or send a text to see how I'm doing?"

He sat across from me with a smile on his face.

"Why are you smiling like that?"

"Because you're in love, and you can't handle him not being here. This is new for you."

"Ugh. I know. This isn't me, and you know it."

"I know it's not, but I've never seen you in love before. Listen, just because he hasn't called or sent a text doesn't mean he isn't thinking about you. Guys are just different when it comes to that stuff. It's not untypical behavior for us. You need to remember he's the CEO of a capital firm. I can't even imagine how busy he is, especially when he's been MIA from New York. He probably has a lot of shit to catch up on and do before he comes back to California. Don't stress about it. You'll hear from him soon enough. Until then, you just do you because I know how busy you are. That's all you need to think about right now. He'll be back and in your bed soon enough." He smirked.

"You're right. Thanks, friend. I guess I just needed a little pep talk. I would have talked to Julia—well—you saw her. She would have just told me to grow the fuck up." I laughed.

"Yeah. Those two can't do or think about anyone or anything else right now."

CHAPTER 22

*J*enni

I'd had a long but very productive day, and when I stepped through the doors of my apartment building, it was eight o'clock.

"Good evening, Jenni." Stuart, my doorman, smiled.

"Good evening, Stuart."

"A package came for you this afternoon."

He reached behind him, grabbed it, and handed it to me.

"Thank you."

I took it up to my apartment and set it on the island. Kicking off my shoes, I grabbed a bottle of wine and poured some into a glass. Grabbing a knife, I slid it through the top, opened the box, and took out a package that was beautifully wrapped in pink and gold paper with a large satin bow. After taking the wrapping off, I placed my hand over my mouth when I saw a box of chocolates from Edwart Chocolatier in Paris. Lifting the lid from off the chocolates, I put a piece in my mouth and just about died. Sitting at the bottom of the original box was a white envelope. Removing the card, I read it with a smile on my face.

I wanted you to have something to enjoy while I'm gone.
You better Facetime me when you get this.
Love, Shaun

Looking at the clock, it was after eleven pm in New York. Oh well, he told me to Facetime him. Picking up my phone, I pulled up his number and hit Facetime. Within seconds, his sexy face was on my screen.

"It's about fucking time." He grinned.

"I just got home. Thank you for the chocolates. They're my favorite."

"You're welcome. How are you?"

"I'm good. You?" I tried to act casual and as if I didn't miss him.

"Busy, stressed, tired."

"Welcome to the club. I spent the day conducting interviews and setting up shop."

"Anyone good?"

"Yeah. I know exactly whom I'm going to offer the positions to."

"Good. How is everyone else doing?"

"They're good. Sam and Julia are finding parenthood quite the challenge."

"I bet. It can't be easy dealing with two babies at the same time."

"My mom is going to be spending about a week there to help out and give her some tips and tricks."

"That's good." He set his phone on his dresser and took off his shirt.

My legs tightened as I stared at his muscular body and tightened, even more, when he stripped out of his pants. He grabbed his phone and climbed into bed.

"It's good to see you, Jenni. I mean that."

"It's good to see you too, Shaun." The corners of my mouth curved upward.

"What are you going to do now that you're home?" he asked.

"Take a bath, relax, and finish up a design for a dress I'm in the middle of."

"A bath, eh?" His lips formed a smirk. "How about you take me with you?"

I swallowed hard as I felt a twitch down below.

"Okay." I smiled. "If you insist."

"Oh, I do."

I walked into the bathroom, flipped on the light, and set my phone up against the back of the counter. After starting the water, I stared at him as I slowly stripped out of my clothes.

"You're killing me, Jen." He stroked his hard cock.

~

J stopped at Simon's house the following day before heading to the studio.

"Morning." Grace smiled as I stepped through the door. "Coffee?"

I glanced at my watch. "Sure. I have time for a quick cup."

"Hey, good morning." Simon walked into the kitchen. "Did you stay at Shaun's last night?"

"Morning. No. I stayed at my place. Why?"

"I don't know. I figured since you were here so early, you did."

Grace eyed me up and down while my coffee brewed.

"Spill it, sister."

"What?" I cocked my head at her.

"You know what I'm talking about." She smirked as she handed me my coffee.

"What?" Simon asked as he looked at me.

I grinned. "How did you know?"

"Girl, we women always know. You know that."

"What? What is she talking about?" Simon asked.

"Shaun and I had Facetime sex." I bit down on my bottom lip.

"Oh my God! Over Facetime? I thought it was just over the phone. Shit. That had to be so hot."

"It was incredibly hot."

"Why don't we ever have Facetime sex?" Grace asked Simon as she glanced over at him.

"Because we're always together!"

Grace shrugged her shoulders.

"Then maybe I'll have to take a trip." She smiled.

"You're not going anywhere. I'd much rather have sex when we're together."

"You have no idea what you're missing." I pointed at him. "It takes things to a whole new level."

He stood there and shook his head at me.

"What? You're the one who chose to listen in. You know what we girls talk about when we get together. Anyway, I have to get to the studio." I walked over and kissed Simon's cheek. "You really need to try it." I gave him a wink. "Bye, Grace." I grinned.

"I want details later!" she shouted as I walked out the door.

When I arrived at the studio, Wes, the man who impressed me yesterday, was waiting outside the door.

"I am so sorry I'm late." I climbed out of my car, grabbed my bag, and ran up to the door. "I needed to make a stop at my friend's house for a minute, and we got sidetracked talking about Facetime sex."

"Oh." His brow arched. "Isn't that so hot?"

"Yes!" My eyes lit up.

Unlocking the door, we stepped inside.

"Have you?" A smirk crossed my lips.

"I sure have. I will admit I'm a little bit free with that and guys I meet online."

"Nothing wrong with that." I smiled. "Anyway, thank you for coming in for a second interview. I like you, Wes, and I think we have a connection."

"We do have a connection, Jenni." A grin crossed his face. "I felt it the second I saw you, and if I weren't gay, I'd totally date you."

I smiled at him. "Aw, you're sweet, but I'm taken."

"I have no doubt you are. Any straight man would be a fool not to get with you."

"Have I mentioned that you're hired?"

"Really?" His face lit up.

"Yes. I called your previous employer, and he had nothing but wonderful things to say about you. Why didn't you go with him to Paris?"

"I wanted to, but I stayed back for a man, and shortly after, things didn't work out."

"I'm sorry." I placed my hand on his shoulder.

"It's okay. I just met someone last week, and we've been hanging out."

"Good for you, Wes!"

"So, who's the lucky man?"

A wide grin crossed my lips. "His name is Shaun, he's an investor in Simply Jenni, and he bought this building for me. I'll Facetime him so I can introduce you. I'm not sure he'll answer, though. He's very busy."

Pulling out my phone, I Facetimed Shaun, and his handsome face appeared on my screen after the first ring.

"Hello there, beautiful." He smiled.

"I wasn't sure if you'd answer."

"You caught me at the right time. I'm getting ready to head into a meeting. What's up?"

"I want you to meet someone. Shaun, this is Wes, my new assistant." I turned the phone to Wes. "Wes, this is Shaun Sterling."

"It's a pleasure to meet you, Mr. Sterling."

"Call me, Shaun. And it's nice to meet you, Wes."

"Call me crazy, but your background doesn't look like Los Angeles."

Shaun chuckled. "That's because I'm at my office in New York. Tell them I'll be right there. Listen, I need to get into my meeting. I'll talk to you later."

"Bye." I smiled as I bit down on my bottom lip.

"Behave yourself today." His brow arched. "Bye."

I ended the call and let out a long sigh.

"Okay, missy. That man is hot as fuck!"

"He is, isn't he?" I swooned.

CHAPTER 23

TWO WEEKS LATER

*S*haun
    I'd sent Jenni the box of chocolates from Paris because she was mad at me, and for the first time in my life, I cared when a woman was angry at something I'd said or done. Usually, I didn't because I never liked anyone enough to give a shit. But with Jenni, I did, and as hard as I tried not to be in contact with her while I was in New York, I couldn't. I missed her, and I hated myself for feeling that way. I hated that I missed her smile, her voice, her quirky ways, and the sex. God, I missed being buried deep inside her and holding her in my arms.

I was leaving New York two days earlier than planned. My work here was finished for now, and I wanted to get back to California, but I didn't tell her I was coming because I wanted it to be a surprise.

As soon as my plane landed, I climbed into the limousine the car service sent. Pulling my phone from my pocket, I sent Jenni a text message.

"Hey, gorgeous. How's your day going?"

"Hi. *It's going great. The delivery guys are here delivering my desk.*"

"*That's great. I can't wait to see it when I get back. I have to run. Talk to you later.*"

"*Facetime later?*"

A smile crossed my lips. "*Of course.*"

I stepped through the studio door, and I was shocked at how quickly she put everything together. Hearing voices coming from upstairs, I left my suitcase by the door and quietly walked up and saw her and Wes in her office looking at her desk.

"It looks great," I spoke as I stood outside the doorway.

Jenni whipped her head around, and the moment she saw me, she ran into my arms.

"Oh my God! What are you doing here?"

"I decided to come back a couple of days early." I tightly hugged her.

"I'm happy you did." She smiled as she broke our embrace. "I can't believe you didn't tell me."

My lips met hers for a moment.

"I wanted to surprise you. Are you surprised?"

"I'm so surprised." She hugged me.

"Wes." I gave him a nod.

"Hello, Shaun. Welcome back to Cali."

"Thank you. The place looks great. When is everyone starting?"

"Tomorrow. Wes has been such a godsend and has helped me so much already."

"Good." I smiled. "Your work here is done. Grab your purse, and let's get out of here. You're all mine for the rest of the day and night."

The corners of her mouth curved upward into a beautiful smile.

"Okay. Give me a second."

"I'll be waiting downstairs."

Placing my hands in my pants pockets, I went downstairs and looked around. I was proud of what she'd accomplished while I was gone.

"I'm ready." She grinned as she walked down the stairs.

"Key?" I held out my hand.

"All yours." She handed me the key to her car.

After we pulled into the driveway of my house, I grabbed my bags from the back and unlocked the front door. Setting my bags in the foyer, I turned around and swooped Jenni up in my arms. I couldn't wait any longer for the sweet taste of her upon my lips. Our mouths met, and our tongues were reunited with excitement. Carrying her upstairs and to my bedroom, I laid her on the bed and hovered over her.

"Facetime sex was great and all, but nothing beats being able to touch you like this." I ran my hand up her thigh until I reached her panties. "I missed this." I pushed them to the side and dipped my finger inside.

She let out a gasp as she brought my head down until my lips met hers.

I explored her and hit the spot that always made her orgasm. Her soft sensual moans had my cock so hard I thought it was going to explode. Taking the straps of her dress down, I pulled off her dress and tossed it on the floor.

"Do you know what else I missed?" I asked as I pulled off her panties.

"What?"

"This." I spread her legs and brought my mouth to the area that gave me so much pleasure.

She let out a satisfying moan as her fingers gripped the comforter while my tongue teased, and my lips tasted the sweetness of her.

"Oh God, I've missed this," she moaned.

After bringing her to an orgasm a second time, I stood up

and stripped off my clothes. Jenni sat up, scooted to the edge of the bed, and wrapped her lips around my cock. I threw my head back in total bliss and took in the overwhelming sensation her beautiful mouth gave me. I told her I was about to come, and she didn't care. She kept going until I exploded, and the rush of ecstasy tore through me. I lifted her head and stared into her eyes as my cock still ached to be inside her. Reaching for my wallet, she grabbed hold of my wrist and slowly shook her head.

"I think we're at the point where we don't need to use a condom. You know I'm on birth control."

"Are you sure?"

"I've never been so sure of anything in my life as I am at this moment."

I climbed on the bed and hovered over her as I ran my hand through her hair and our lips meshed. Pushing inside her, I gasped at the warmth and the wetness that enveloped my cock.

"You feel so good," she whispered.

"You have no idea," I moaned as I thrust in and out of her.

Her legs tightened around my waist as her breath exploded and the pressure built. Within moments, I crossed the threshold into pure bliss.

My heart pounded out of my chest as I dropped my body on hers and buried my face into the side of her neck. Pulling out of her, I rolled on my back and turned my head, so I was looking at her.

"Welcome home." The corners of her mouth curved upward.

I smiled as I brought my hand to her cheek and softly stroked it.

"It's good to be back here."

"Sebastian is having the family for dinner at the restaurant tonight. It'll be Julia and Sam's first outing with the babies. And since you're back, you're coming."

"I am?" I arched my brow.

"Yes. Everyone will be happy to see you."

"I don't want to intrude on a family dinner."

"Please. You're practically family now that we're seeing each other. Plus, they all like you. It'll be fun."

"Okay." I smiled at her. "I'll go."

hile she was in the bathroom fixing her hair, I walked out onto the patio and stared at the blue ocean water as I took in the sound of the waves crashing against the shore. It felt good to be back here. Not only because I missed her, but because everything was falling into place exactly as I planned it.

CHAPTER 24

Shaun

"Welcome home, neighbor," Simon said as he walked over. "It's nice to see that wall gone."

"Yeah. It is." I smiled as we shook hands.

"How was New York?"

"It was good and very productive."

"Jenni didn't tell us you were coming back today. We're having dinner tonight at Emilia's. Join us."

"Jenni didn't know. I wasn't supposed to be back until Sunday evening, but I came back early to surprise her. She invited me to dinner tonight. Are you sure it's okay? I don't want to intrude on your family gathering."

"You're more than welcome." He patted my back. Now that you and Jen are seeing each other and you're our new neighbor, you're invited to all our family gatherings." He smiled.

"Thanks, Simon. That means a lot. Especially since I don't have any family."

"Consider us your family then."

"Hey, you." Jenni smiled as she stepped out on the patio.

"Look who I found standing here," Simon said.

"Isn't it great he's back?"

"It is. I have to run. I'll see you both at the restaurant." He gave us a wink and walked back to his house.

Jenni wrapped her arms around me from behind, and I brought my hands up and gripped them as I thought about what Simon said when he told me to consider them family.

~

"Welcome back, man." Sebastian smiled as we shook hands.

"Yeah. Welcome back." Stefan placed his hand on my back.

"Thanks. It's good to be back in California."

"Scotch?" Sebastian asked.

"Sure."

"I'll go grab one," he spoke as he walked away.

"Sam finished the design for the condos," Stefan spoke.

"Great. I can't wait to see it."

"You're going to love it. He really outdid himself with the design."

"Hi, Shaun."

"Hey, Lily." I smiled as I patted her head.

"Welcome back."

"Thank you."

"The babies are here!" she exclaimed as she ran over to Sam and Julia when they walked in.

Following behind was my father, Celeste, and my baby sister Nora. I brought my glass of scotch up to my lips as I stared at him.

"Hello, Shaun." My father smiled as he walked over and extended his hand.

"Hello, Henry."

"How was New York?"

"It was good."

"I'm sorry. What is it you do again besides being an investor in Jenni's company?"

"I'm the CEO and owner of Sterling Capital Corp."

"Nice. Is it a family-owned business?"

"No. I started it when I was twenty-one after I graduated at the top of my class from Yale."

"Impressive. If you don't mind me asking, what is your net worth?"

"Dad." Stefan's brows furrowed. "That's rude."

"We're all businessmen here, and it is public information."

"It doesn't mean he wants to talk about it!"

"It's fine, Stefan." I glanced over at him and then back at my father.

"Currently, my net worth is fifteen billion dollars. But it will be on the rise once I take over a competitor."

"Impressive." The corners of Henry's mouth curved upward. "And you did all that on your own?"

"My uncle moved in with my mother and me when I was thirteen. He had just lost everything in his divorce and had nowhere else to go. With the little money he had, he started making investments. Some were good, but a majority of them were not. I studied the market and saw the potential to make a lot of money, so I helped him. I told him what to invest in, when, and I told him when to sell. In return, he gave me a percentage of his earnings. I saved every dime of that money, got my shit together, went to Yale on a full-ride scholarship, found a couple of investors, and started my company."

"You're a brilliant man."

"According to the intellectual quotient tests, I have an IQ of 150."

"Damn," Stefan said. "You're like a genius."

"Nice." Henry smiled as he slowly nodded his head. "So, who was the smart one in your family? Your mother or father?"

"Must have been my father, but I wouldn't really know since I'd never met him."

"You grew up without a father?" His eye narrowed at me.

"I did. According to my mother, he was a stranger she'd met at a bar and had a one-night stand with." I stared into his eyes.

Jenni walked over and hooked her arm around mine. "It's time to eat. Let's go sit down."

After dinner, everyone was starting to leave the restaurant.

"Hey," Sam said as he walked over.

"Drinks on the patio at my house when we get back. You better be there."

"Sounds good to me." I smiled.

When we left the restaurant, I parked my car at home, and then Jenni and I walked over to Sam's house.

"I'm going to go inside with the girls." Jenni reached up and kissed my lips. "Have fun with the guys."

"Thanks, babe."

She stood there and stared at me with a wide grin splayed across her face.

"What?" I chuckled.

"You called me 'babe.'"

"Did I?" I gave her a wink and walked back to the patio where my four brothers were sitting.

Sam handed me a glass of scotch when I took a seat next to Sebastian.

"Listen, Shaun," Sam said. "Stefan told us about how our father grilled you at the restaurant. I'm sorry about that."

"Nah. Don't be. It's all good."

"Sometimes, he has no tact." Simon shook his head. "And

he can be difficult to get along with unless you agree with his views."

"Yeah. He can be a real asshole," Sebastian said.

"Can be?" Stefan laughed.

"Well, the only thing I can say is you're lucky you had him around when you were growing up. He must have done something right because the four of you are pretty great."

"Thanks, man," Sam said. "But we're not great because of him. We had each other."

"Yeah. It wasn't easy growing up with our parents. Always in and out of relationships, married, divorced, married, divorced," Stefan said.

"The four of us were pretty fucked up when it came to women," Sebastian said. "When we were younger, the four of us made a pact."

"A pact?"

"No women, no relationships, and no love. Only sex."

"Umm. It looks to me like all that has changed." I gave them a smirk.

"Sam was the first one who broke the pact when he met Julia. Then I broke it with Alex. Sebastian broke it with Emilia, and our boy Simon jumped on board when he met Grace."

"We realized we weren't our parents, and as scary as it was loving them, we had to let go of the fear," Sam said.

"What are you five talking about out here?" Grace smiled as she took a seat on Simon's lap.

"Guy talk, babe. No women allowed."

"Is that so?" Her brow arched. "Did you really just say that? Did you?"

"Come on, babe. You know I was kidding." He kissed her lips.

"That's what I thought."

I couldn't help but laugh. The sliding door opened, and

Jenni, Alex, Julia, and Emilia all stepped onto the patio. I could tell both Jenni and Emilia were drunk.

"Hey, sexy," Jenni said as she sat down on my lap and kissed my lips.

"You smell and taste like lemons." I smirked.

"We were doing a few lemon drop shots in the house. Want one?"

"No. I think it's time we go back to my house." I placed my arms under her legs and stood up.

"We're going surfing in the morning. Meet us out there," Simon said.

"Maybe I will. I haven't had a chance to test out the new surfboard yet." I smiled.

"Great. We'll be down there around seven."

I carried Jenni back to my house and took her right upstairs. Her lips were all over my neck, and I was getting harder by the second.

"I love you," she whispered in my ear.

My heart leaped into my throat.

When I laid her down on the bed, she passed out. After removing her clothes, I pulled back the covers, placed her under them, and tucked her in. Sitting on the edge of the bed, I ran the back of my hand down her cheek as she slept.

"You can't love me, Jenni. You just can't."

I closed my eyes for a moment and then went downstairs and poured myself a scotch.

CHAPTER 25

*S*haun

Before I left to meet my brothers, I checked on Jenni one last time. She was sleeping peacefully, so I grabbed my surfboard and headed down to the beach.

"You made it." Stefan smiled.

"Sam's not here yet?"

"He's not coming. The twins were up all night."

"Ah. Poor guy."

We put our boards in the water and paddled out.

"By the way, we're having a birthday party at my house next week for our dad, and we're hoping you'll come with Jenni," Sebastian said.

"Thanks. I'm sure it'll be fun." I smiled at him.

We surfed, talked, and had a good time.

"You're pretty good." Simon patted my back.

"Thanks. You guys are a lot better than I am."

"We grew up surfing," Stefan said. "Don't worry. Stick with us, and you'll get better."

I walked back over to my house, and when I opened the

sliding door, I saw Jenni standing in front of the coffee maker.

"Morning," I spoke.

"Shh. No talking until I've had coffee."

I let out a light chuckle as she took her cup and went out to the patio.

After taking a shower and getting dressed, I made a coffee and joined Jenni outside. I needed to know if she remembered what she'd said to me last night.

"Is it okay to talk now?" I asked with a smirk as I sat down next to her.

"Yes." She glanced over at me with a smile. "I've taken two aspirin, had two cups of coffee, and I'm good to go. By the way, did we have sex last night?"

"What do you remember about last night?" I asked.

"The last thing I remember was you carrying me to the house."

"That's all you remember?"

"Yeah. Oh my God, what did I do?"

The corners of my mouth curved upward as I felt a sigh of relief.

"I carried you up the stairs, undressed you, and tucked you into bed."

"So, we didn't have sex?"

"No. You were passed out cold." I took a sip of my coffee.

"Sorry about that."

"Don't apologize. We all get like that from time to time." I gave her a wink.

"How was your surf with the boys?"

"It was great. I had a lot of fun. Sebastian told me about their father's birthday party next week."

"Oh yeah. I forgot to mention that to you. You will be my date, right?"

"Of course. I wouldn't miss it for the world." I leaned over and kissed her lips.

∾

One Week Later

I sat behind my desk in my home office and held the letter my mother had written in my hand. I came to California intending to hate my brothers even more than I already had because they existed. If they didn't, my father would never have abandoned us. But I couldn't hate them. They were remarkable men, and they didn't have a clue as to what Henry had done. They were innocent bystanders in all of this, and I prayed to God they would still accept me when they found out the truth about who I really was.

I planned to go after Kind Design & Architecture. A careful and well-thought-out plan I devised. But after meeting my brothers and getting to know them, I couldn't go through with it. My father, on the other hand, was a different story. I was more than ready to make him pay for what he'd done.

"Are you ready to go?" Jenni asked as she stood in the doorway of my office.

She had startled me from my thoughts, and I quickly folded the letter in my hand and slipped it in the top drawer of my desk. I'd lock it up later.

"I am more than ready." I smiled at her as I stood up from my seat.

Walking past her, I kissed her forehead.

"What was that for?" A grin crossed her lips.

"Do I need a reason to kiss any part of your body?"

Her grin widened. "No."

"Then just know that when I do, there is no reason, and only because I can't help myself when you're in my presence." I gave her a wink.

We walked over to Sebastian's, and when we stepped inside, we noticed everyone was outside.

"We've arrived." Jenni smiled as we stepped out the sliding door.

I looked around for Barb and didn't see her, which was good. I wasn't in the mood to have to deal with her bullshit today.

"Hey, man." Sam, Stefan, and Simon smiled as they walked over.

"Hey." I tucked my hands in my pants pockets. "What a turnout."

"Yeah. My dad invited some friends and forgot to tell me," Sebastian spoke. "Beer or something stronger?"

"Beer is fine. We can save the stronger stuff for later." The corners of my mouth curved upward.

"Damn right." He patted my back.

"If you'll excuse me, I'm going to use the bathroom."

"Yeah. Of course. You know where it's at."

Walking in the house, I approached the bathroom on the first level and saw the closed door. Leaning against the wall, I waited for whoever was inside to finish. When the door opened, Henry walked out, and it looked like he was out of breath.

"Henry, are you okay?" I asked.

"I'm fine, Shaun."

"You don't look well."

"I'm just tired. Nora has been keeping us up at night." He gave a small smile.

"I'm sure she has. Happy birthday."

"Thank you. I'm going to head outside. I'll see you out there."

I gave him a nod and stepped inside the bathroom. Something was off with him, and I didn't think Nora had anything to do with it.

CHAPTER 26

*J*enni

"Here you go." Alex handed me a watermelon margarita.

She always seemed to be the designated bartender at our parties.

"Thank you." I took a sip. "Wow. Delicious."

"How are things with you and Shaun? I see you're practically living at his house," Grace said.

"Are you being a nosy neighbor?"

"Yes, I am, and I'm not sorry." She smirked.

I let out a laugh.

"Things with Shaun are amazing. I can honestly say I've never been this happy in my life. He has totally changed my views on relationships. And I am happy to say that he has checked off every single box on my perfect guy list."

"I'm so happy for you." Julia hooked her arm around me. "Shaun is a great guy, and I couldn't ask for a better man for my sister."

"Aw, sis. Thank you. I know we've talked about it before,

but how do you deal with Sam's obsession with cleanliness and organization?"

"Trust me. I don't think anyone can be like Sam."

"I wouldn't be so sure about that," I said. "The other day, while I was brushing my teeth, some water splashed on the mirror and left some spots. Shaun was at the sink next to mine shaving, and he glanced over and said, 'The glass cleaner and cloth is under the sink.' He literally made me clean it right then and there."

"Oh my God, that is one of Sam's biggest pet peeves. You learn to roll with it because you love him, flaws and all." She smiled.

"Speaking of love," Emilia said. "Have the two of you said the three magic words yet?"

"No." I let out a sigh. "And I'm not going to say it until he tells me first."

"Why?" Alex asked. "There's nothing wrong with a woman saying it first."

"Really?" I arched my brow as I looked at Julia, Alex, and Emilia. "Have you forgotten that I was nursing each one of you from a broken heart when you all told the guys how you felt?"

"Oh shit. Yeah." Emilia frowned.

"Well, I didn't have that issue with Simon."

"Only because he practically kicked you out of his house before you could tell him." Julia laughed.

"True. That is very true." Grace slowly nodded her head, and we all laughed.

Sam walked in holding Lena and handed her over to Julia.

"I think she wants to eat."

"Okay. What about Lorelei?"

"She's sound asleep in Shaun's arms."

I glanced out the sliding door and saw Lorelei sleeping

peacefully in Shaun's arms. A smile crossed my lips as my heart completely melted.

"He looks good holding a baby." Grace walked over and stood next to me.

"He certainly does."

"Does he want children?" she asked.

"I don't know. We've never talked about kids. I know his childhood wasn't so great. You know how that affects some guys."

"Yep. I know." She sighed. "But he seems like he turned out just fine. I foresee a beautiful future for the two of you."

"I hope so. I really love him, Grace, and I'm scared shitless."

She hooked her arm around me.

"I know you are, Jen." She gave me a gentle squeeze. "But I truly believe Shaun is different, and I know he's in love with you. I see it. He's not going to hurt you."

~

Shaun

Lorelei had woken up, and I handed her off to Sam so Julia could feed her. Sitting next to me was Lily, and she was holding Henry while making silly faces at him.

"You're a great big sister," I said to her.

"Thanks. I know he's going to need me to protect him when he's older."

"Yes, he will."

"You don't have any brothers or sisters?" she asked.

"Umm. No. I grew up an only child."

"You must have been lonely. I know sometimes I was before Henry."

"I was at times."

"Why didn't your mom and dad have any more kids?"

"Well, my mother never married, and I never knew my father."

"That's hard." She placed her small hand on my arm. "My mother left me with my dad when I was three, and she never came back. So, I can relate."

"I'm sorry, Lily."

"It's okay. My dad was always there for me like I'm sure your mom was."

I gave her a small smile, and when I glanced over, I saw Henry staring at us.

"She was, kiddo."

"Maybe you can find your dad."

"Hey, what's going on over here." Stefan smiled and then looked at me with wide eyes. "Why don't you give me your brother and go inside and help Emilia put the candles on Grandpa's birthday cake."

"Okay." She handed Henry to him. "Bye, Shaun."

"Bye, Lily."

"Sorry. I heard what she said."

"It's okay. It seems me and her have a lot in common."

"Yeah. Except her mother got caught up with some bad people and drugs."

"Well, if you ask me, you did a great job raising her."

"Thanks, man. I couldn't have done it without the help of my family or Alex. When she walked into my life, Lily was at her worst. Her previous nanny, who was the closest thing to her mother, got sick and had to move to Maine. Then when Alex came along, Lily was not having it. But Alex worked her magic and her way into Lily's heart. I knew right then and there she was the woman I was meant to spend the rest of my life with. How are things going with you and Jenni?"

"Things are great. No complaints."

"Hi." Jenni walked over and wrapped her arms around me from behind.

"Hi, gorgeous." I smiled as I turned my head, and her lips met mine.

"Okay, everyone, it's time to sing happy birthday to the birthday boy." Emilia smiled.

She set the cake down in front of Henry.

"Hold on a second!" Sebastian said. "Don't sing yet."

He ran inside the house and grabbed his guitar.

"Okay. Ready. And a one, and a two, and a—"

We all started to sing happy birthday while he strummed the chords. I sat there trying not to choke on the words as I sang them. Henry had a smile on his face, but it didn't seem genuine. He seemed preoccupied. After we finished singing, he asked Lily to help him blow out the candles. After he blew out a few, I could tell he was short of breath, just like he was when he came out of the bathroom.

"Hey, is your dad okay?" I asked Stefan.

"I think so. Why?"

"It just seemed like it was hard for him to blow out those candles."

"He was probably doing that on purpose for Lily so she could blow them all out."

"Yeah. Probably."

Celebrating my father's birthday was difficult. But I needed to be there to watch him, study him, and see how much of an asshole he still was. When it came to him, anger still clouded me like a circling puff of smoke that never dissipated.

"Do you want some cake?" Jenni asked.

"No, thanks. I'm still full from all the food Sebastian made."

"Are you sure?" She grinned as she held the plate up to me. "It's amazing."

"How about I take a piece home where I can eat it in private." My lips formed a smirk.

"I'm going to go cut you a piece or two—hell, make it three and set it aside to take home." Her eyes lit up.

"You go do that." I gave her a wink.

CHAPTER 27

*S*haun

I placed frosting on various parts of her body first and then made my way up, starting at her inner thigh.

"You were right. This frosting is delicious." I looked up at her with a smile as my tongue slid up her abdomen.

"Oh God," she moaned as her fingers ran through my hair.

My tongue made its way from her abdomen to her nipples that were covered in frosting. Wrapping my lips around each of them, I sucked most of the frosting off and used my tongue to circle them and lick off the rest while my fingers were inside her. I could feel the pulsing sensation as she let out a loud moan and her body shook as she orgasmed. The warm wetness dripped from her, and I couldn't wait any longer. I moved my body up and hovered over her until my throbbing cock was between her legs and at her opening. With one push, I thrust inside and threw my head back at the sensation that overtook me. She was on fire, and it felt incredible. Her nails dug into my back as I moved in and out of her, trying to hold back the come that wanted to escape.

Pulling out, I rolled her on her stomach, grabbed her hips, and lifted her to meet my cock as I pounded into her at a rapid pace. Low, rough grunts escaped my lips while high-pitched moans came from her. Reaching around the front of her, I stroked her clit, which sent her into a full-blown orgasm, making my cock spasm out of control and explode inside her.

Gripping her hips, I stilled myself as I tried to catch my breath while Jenni lay there trying to do the same. I pulled out and fell on my back, placing my hand over my racing heart. Still on her stomach, she glanced over at me with a smile on her face as she put her hand over mine.

"Damn. That was—"

"You don't have to say it. Trust me. I know." The corners of my mouth curved upward.

"I need to take a shower and wash off the stickiness of the frosting. I'll be right back." She sat up and kissed my lips.

"I would join you, but—"

"No need to explain. It's best you don't."

While Jenni was in the shower, I grabbed my phone from the nightstand and noticed I had a voicemail from Teddy Cooper at Cooper Capital.

"You're a fucking snake, Shaun. Going public with Grieger's stock fucked me and my company. But you knew it would, and that's why you did it. I swear to God I will fight with every breath I have left to keep you out. This is my company! Go to hell, Sterling, and fuck you!"

I let out a laugh as I listened to it. Pulling up Adam's number, I sent him a text message.

"Cooper is pissed as hell. Make sure I get a seat on that board. Big changes are coming."

"I know he is, and I'm already on it."

Jenni emerged from the bathroom with a towel wrapped

around her. Walking over to the dresser drawer where she kept a couple of nightshirts here, I stopped her.

"What are you doing?"

"Getting a nightshirt out."

"No. Drop the towel and get in here naked. I want to feel your clean, soft body against mine all night."

"Are you going to behave yourself?" Her brow arched from across the room.

"Only if you want me to be. But I can't make any promises."

With a smile, she dropped the towel from her body, and it landed on the floor, making me cringe at the thought of it staying there all night. As she climbed into bed, I climbed out.

"I need to use the bathroom. I'll be right back."

Walking over to where the towel sat, I picked it up and went into the bathroom.

"Really, Shaun?" I heard her shout.

"What? It was on the way to the bathroom," I shouted back. "Besides, it's not good for the floor to leave a wet towel on it."

I climbed back into bed and held out my arm as she snuggled against me.

"You have issues," she spoke.

"How is picking up a wet towel from the floor an issue?"

"It just is. Go to sleep." She pressed her lips against my chest.

"Good night, Jenni."

"Good night, Shaun."

The following morning, I got up early, made a cup of coffee, and stepped onto the patio. The brightness of the morning sun had already warmed the air. Looking down towards Henry's house, I saw him standing by the water, so I took my coffee and walked over to him.

"Good morning." I smiled.

"No. It's not a good morning," he grumbled.

"What's wrong?"

"I woke up this morning to an investment that majorly crashed. My stockbroker couldn't sell fast enough."

"Wow. I'm sorry to hear that. Don't tell me it was Grieger."

"It was. Some asshole went public with the stock, and it totally fucked me, and I lost millions. The worst part is that I had some of the company's shares invested. Now, Kind Design & Architecture could suffer as well. I don't know how to tell the boys. Please don't say anything to them until I figure it out."

"I won't. What are you going to do?"

"I don't know. I'm waiting for my financial guy to call me. I need to go lay down. I hope you have a better day than I am."

"Thanks, Henry. I'm sure everything will work out."

I walked away with a smile on my face as I brought my cup up to my lips. As I made my way back to the house, I saw Jenni sitting on the patio with a cup of coffee in her hand.

"Why are you up already?" I asked her, and I leaned down and kissed her lips.

"I woke up, and you weren't there. I was very disappointed, Mr. Sterling."

"I knew I wore you out last night, and I wanted you to get all the rest you could. Don't forget there are two more pieces of cake left."

"You're so thoughtful." She grinned. "I saw you talking to Henry. How is he this morning?"

"He's in a bit of a funk. Some investment of his went bad overnight."

"Shit. Poor guy."

"Listen, Jen. I need to fly to New York for a meeting, and I want you to come with me."

"Really?" Her eyes lit up with excitement.

"Yes. We'll stay at my penthouse and spend a couple of days in the city."

"When?"

"Our flight leaves in three hours."

"Three hours! What? When did you book the flight?"

"Last night."

"And you're just telling me now? I have to go home and pack and—oh my God! There's not enough time?"

"We have plenty of time. I'm going to get dressed and throw a bag together, and we'll go to your apartment so you can pack. But pack light. We'll only be gone a couple of days."

CHAPTER 28

*J*enni

"This is your idea of packing light?" Shaun said as he wheeled my large suitcase for me. "When I said 'light,' I meant a carry-on bag. Not a large suitcase, small suitcase, plus a carry-on bag. We're only going for two days. How much could you possibly need?"

"A girl needs options, Shaun."

I heard him let out a sigh.

After checking my luggage and going through security, we had to run to our gate, for they were already boarding. The flight attendant was getting ready to shut the doors when we reached it.

"Wait!" I shouted as I held up my boarding pass.

"You're lucky you made it on time."

"I always do." I grinned as I looked at Shaun, and he gave me a stern look.

I let out a breath as we took our seats in first class.

"Do you know how stressed that just made me?" Shaun said. "If you hadn't packed so much, we wouldn't have had to check your luggage, and we would have had plenty of time to get to our gate."

"Listen, you're the one that sprung this last-minute trip on me. 'Hey, Jen, guess what? We're leaving for New York in three hours.'"

"So, it's my fault?"

"Yes. As a matter of fact, it is." My brow raised. "You need to give a girl some notice."

"I did. I gave you three hours' notice, and I told you to pack light."

I sat there and narrowed my eyes at him. "Actually, I did pack light."

He inhaled a sharp breath and slowly closed his eyes.

"It's best you keep whatever you're going to say to your-self." I patted his arm.

When we arrived in New York and stepped off the plane, Shaun threw his carry-on over his shoulder.

"Don't forget we have to stop at baggage claim," I said.

"How could I forget?" He glanced over at me.

By the time we arrived at baggage claim, my luggage was already coming around. I grabbed the smaller suitcase while Shaun grabbed my larger one.

"My driver is waiting for us on the second level," he said.

We took the elevator up to the second level, and when we stepped off, an older gentleman was waiting for us.

"Welcome back, Shaun."

"Thank you, Miles. This is Jenni. Jenni, my driver, Miles."

"It's nice to meet you, Jenni." He smiled as he took my luggage and my carry-on bag from me.

"It's nice to meet you too, Miles."

We climbed into the back of the limousine while Miles stored my luggage and both our carry-on bags in the trunk. When he pulled up to the tall building on the Upper East Side, Shaun climbed out first, and I followed with the help of his hand. After Miles had retrieved our luggage, we wheeled them inside and stepped into the elevator.

"Private keyed entrance?" I smirked.

"Of course." He smiled.

When the doors opened, I stepped into the grand foyer.

"Wow. I love this." I smiled as I looked around.

"Thanks, and welcome to my New York home."

I walked over to the floor-to-ceiling windows and stared out at the fantastic view of the city.

"I don't think I'd ever get tired of looking at this view."

Shaun walked over and wrapped his arms around me from behind.

"It's nice, but I like the ocean view better."

"Are you still mad at me for packing too much?" I tilted my head back and stared up at him.

"No. The one thing I learned today was that I can't stay mad at you for very long." He kissed the tip of my nose.

"That's too bad." I pouted.

"Why?"

"Because I was hoping that you were going to punish me once we got here."

"Oh." His brow raised. "In that case, I am furious at you for not listening to me."

He picked me up and threw me over his shoulder.

"And now, I'm going to take you upstairs to my bedroom, and you're going to do exactly as I say." He slapped my ass as he carried me up the stairs. "Do you understand me?"

"Maybe you should do that again. I'm not sure I understand."

He slapped my ass again, and I smiled.

*S*haun

Adam and I took the elevator up to Cooper Capital. We had a last-minute meeting scheduled with him, and it wasn't going to be pretty.

"Good morning, Mr. Sterling. Mr. Cooper is in the conference room waiting for you."

Teddy and his team sat there glaring at us when Adam and I stepped into the conference room.

"Teddy." I gave him a nod.

"Shaun." He took in a sharp breath.

"Listen, I can make all your problems go away. You know that."

"What I know is you're a dirty fucking snake."

"I've been called worse."

"There's no way I'm letting you buy out my family's company. My great grandfather started this company with nothing but a few bucks to his name."

"You're in debt up to your eyeballs, Teddy, and you've mismanaged the company after your father died. You've offered investors deals to get them to sign on that you can't deliver. Your name and reputation are going down the toilet. Let me stop it before it's too late and you and your family lose everything."

"We were doing fine until you made Grieger stock public, you son-of-a-bitch!"

"You weren't doing fine, and I have the documents to prove it! Sterling Capital will get you and your family out of this mess, and you and your sister will keep your seats on the board. The only change will be that Sterling Cap takes over ownership and management. You have forty-eight hours. If I don't hear from you, you're done, and you know it. Put your hatred for me and your pride aside and take what I'm offering you."

He sat there glaring at me from across the table.

"You really don't have a choice, Teddy." I stood up. "Forty-eight hours." Adam and I walked out of the conference room.

"Do you think he'll accept?" Adam asked as we walked to the elevator.

"He'll accept."

"What are your plans with Grieger now that you're the majority shareholder?"

"Besides taking the millions that my father lost?" I smirked.

CHAPTER 29

ONE MONTH LATER

*J*enni

"The two of you still haven't said the words yet?" Wes asked.

"Not yet." I pouted as I stood back and looked at the dress I had designed.

"Girl, what the fuck?"

"I know. I've been thinking about it a lot lately, and I know he loves me."

"Of course, he does. Who wouldn't? You're amazing." He hooked his arm around me.

"Thanks. I don't know why he hasn't told me yet."

"He's probably nervous. You're a bold gal. You say it first."

"You think?" I bit down on my bottom lip as I glanced over at him.

"Yes."

"And what if he says nothing back?"

"I don't think that's going to happen, but if he doesn't, then maybe you need to rejudge the validity of the relationship. I mean, there are a couple of reasons why he might not have said it yet."

"Like?" I walked over and grabbed the sleeve of the dress and held it up.

"Maybe he isn't ready to fulfill the expectations that come with the words. Maybe saying it would put too much pressure on him."

"That's dumb."

"I agree, but some guys are like that. I think you just need to take the leap and go for it. What's the worst that can happen besides him saying that he doesn't love you back. Which he won't!" Wes pointed at me. "I see the way you two are, and I can tell he's in love with you."

"You know what? You're right. I'm cooking dinner for him tonight at his place, so I'll tell him after dinner and a bottle of wine." I grinned.

~

"Hey, you," Simon spoke as he opened the sliding door and walked in.

"Hi."

"I saw your car out there. Where's Shaun?"

"His friend Adam is in town, and they're going over business stuff. He should be home soon." I smiled. "What are you up to?"

"I just wanted to stop by and see how you're doing. It feels like we don't see much of you anymore."

"Aw, you miss me. You're sweet. I've been really busy with work."

"And with Shaun." His lips formed a smirk.

"Yes. Him too." I grinned.

"Anyway, I just want to stop by and say hi." He walked over and kissed my cheek. "Tell Shaun I said hi."

"I will. Tell Grace I said hi."

"I will. Talk to you later."

"Bye, Simon."

As I was in the middle of cooking dinner, my phone rang with an unfamiliar number.

"Hello," I answered and put it on speaker.

"Hello, I'm looking for a Miss Jenni Benton."

"This is she."

"Miss Benton, this is Seymour Klaus. I'm a buyer with Nordstrom, and I'm calling in regards to your fashion line you submitted to us."

My heart started pounding out of my chest.

"Mr. Klaus. It's good to hear from you."

"I've looked over your designs, and I'm very interested. Do you have the line ready for viewing?"

"Yes. There are just a couple more things that need to be done for the last piece."

"I'd love to take a look. Can you bring them to my office?"

"Yes. Yes. Of course."

"Do you have a pen and paper handy? I'll give you the address."

"Umm. Hold on a second."

Looking around the kitchen, I didn't see any, so I went into Shaun's office. Taking a seat at his desk, I opened the top drawer and grabbed a piece of paper and a pen.

"Okay, I'm ready."

He rattled off the address, and I wrote it down. We set the day and time for the meeting, and I ended the call. As I sat there, excitement flowed through me, as did panic. What if he hated the clothes in person? No. I couldn't think like that. Positive thoughts only.

As I was getting up from the chair, I noticed a piece of paper half sticking out from the bottom drawer. It struck me as odd because that wasn't like Shaun to leave it like that. Pulling open the drawer, I noticed it was a handwritten letter. I went to fold it back up and stopped as curiosity got the best of me. One side of my brain was telling me I shouldn't read it, but the other side of my brain was telling me I should. Looking at the signature at the bottom, it was from his mother.

"Shit. Don't do it, Jen. It's personal," I said out loud as I folded it back up.

Then my inside voice started to reason with me. "He'll never know. Just read it, put it back, and forget about it."

Unfolding the letter, I sat back in the chair. As I began reading it, I brought my hand up to my mouth when a sickness roared inside me. Tears filled my eyes and shock paralyzed me.

"What the fuck!" I said as I threw the letter on the desk. "Henry is Shaun's father, and the boys are his brothers?"

I couldn't believe it, and I swallowed the lump in my throat that nearly choked me.

Looking down at the open drawer, I saw a stack of file folders, so I took them out and opened each one of them only to find pictures and information on me, Simon, Stefan, Sebastian, Sam, and Henry. Tears streamed down my face as I flew out of my seat and ran to the bathroom to throw up. I couldn't stop the uncontrollable shaking as a million things ran through my mind. Nothing was a coincidence when it came to him. He carefully planned everything that had to do with the Kind family, including me.

After I was done in the bathroom, I grabbed the letter and the folders and spread them out on the island. My phone pinged and scared the shit out of me. Picking it up, there was a text message from Shaun.

"Hey, beautiful. I'm on my way home now. I should be there in ten minutes."

I didn't respond because I couldn't bring myself to. Instead, I poured a glass of wine and threw it down the back of my throat. Taking a seat on the couch, I brought my knees to my chest and waited for him. I couldn't sit still, so I got up and paced back and forth across the living room. This was all a mistake. It had to be.

I heard his car pull up in the driveway, and instantly, the sick feeling inside me intensified. Walking over to the island, I gripped the marble counter, lowered my head, and took in several deep breaths. The moment the door opened, and he stepped inside, I lifted my head and stared at him.

CHAPTER 30

*J*enni

"Hi." His brows furrowed when he saw me.

"Jenni, what's wrong?" He slowly began to walk towards me as his eyes diverted to the contents on the island.

"What the fuck is all this?" I shouted as I picked up the pictures and the letter.

He put his hands up. "Jenni, calm down. Please."

"Calm down?" I shouted. "You knew all this time that Henry is your father, and those boys are your brothers, and you didn't bother to tell anyone?"

"You don't understand. Let me explain."

"Why is there information on me and a picture of me?" I tried to hold back the tears, but they fell down my face anyway.

"Let's go sit down, and I'll tell you everything."

"No." I shook my head. "I don't want to sit down!"

"Jenni, please."

"DON'T!" I pointed at him. "Don't please me! You are to tell me right now what the fuck is going on and who you really are!" I shouted.

"As you can see by the letter my mother wrote, I had just found out after she died about Henry and my brothers. She lied to me my entire life. I came here to get to know them before I told them the truth."

"Why? Why couldn't you just tell them the truth from the beginning?"

"Because it's not that simple!" he shouted. "I grew up an only child and alone! Now, thirty-three years later, I find out I have a father and four brothers. You have no idea the impact that has on a person. What did you want me to do? Huh? Just walk up to them and say, 'Hey, I'm your brother from an affair your dad had thirty-three years ago when your mother was pregnant with you?' Or walk up to Henry and say, 'Hey, Dad, I'm your fifth son you never knew about?'"

"Yes! It's called the truth, Shaun!"

"You don't understand, Jenni. I hate that man for what he did, and I hate that he chose Barb over my mother. When I found out about Sam, Stefan, Sebastian, and Simon, I was full of rage and anger. I hated them right off the bat because they got to grow up with my father!"

"So, all of this is an act?"

"No. Because when I met them, I felt this instant connection and I couldn't hate them."

I looked down and picked up the picture of me.

"Meeting me wasn't a coincidence, was it?" More tears fell from my eyes. "You planned it all along. Just like you planned to invest in my company. You used me to get to them."

"Jenni." He took a step closer.

"Don't you dare come any closer to me!" I shouted through gritted teeth.

"You want the truth? Here it is. Yes, I planned on using you to get to them, but the one thing I didn't plan on was falling madly in love with you. And you want to know why? Because I never thought I could love anyone."

"You bastard." I slowly shook my head. "Everything from the night we met was nothing but a lie, and I fell for it."

"Jenni, stop and listen to me."

"Meeting Simon and Grace at the hotel was a lie. You were never meeting anyone for a blind date, were you?"

"No." He looked down.

"Coming here for business and buying this house. How the fuck did you get the Bennett's to sell?"

"I offered them an all-cash deal at triple the value, and they jumped at it."

"Who the fuck do you think you are? God? You think because you have billions that you can just do whatever the hell you want at the expense of other people?"

"No. You're wrong!"

"Really, Shaun? Because that's what it seems like! Does anyone else know about this?"

"Barb knows."

"Barb?" My brows furrowed. "How the hell would Barb know?"

"My mother met her in a coffee shop and told her everything about her affair with Henry and that she was pregnant with me. She thought if Barb knew what a cheating bastard Henry was, she'd leave him and go back to her."

"Oh my God." I placed my hands over my face before slamming my fists down on the counter.

"Were you ever going to tell them or me?" I angrily shouted.

"Yes."

"When?! When were you going to?"

"I don't know! But the one thing I do know is that you're the most important person in my life, and I love you." He stepped closer until he was within my reach.

"No." I shook my head. "No, you don't. If you did, you

155

wouldn't have lied to me! I began pounding on his chest as the tears freely fell. "It's all lies! All of it!"

He grabbed hold of my wrists and held them tight.

"Calm down and listen to me."

I struggled to break out of his grip, but he was stronger. He turned me around, wrapped his arms around me from behind, and held me in his grip.

"I love you, Jenni, and we can get through this. I swear to God, I'm telling you the honest truth."

"We will never get through this." I broke free from his grip and turned to face him. "All of this, us, the things we did together, it was all a lie, and I hate you for that. I hate you so much, Shaun Sterling!"

I grabbed my purse and slung it over my shoulder.

"You better fucking tell them who you are, or I will!" I ran out the door and to my car.

"Jenni, wait!" Shaun ran after me.

"Stay the fuck away from me, and don't ever talk to me again! Do you understand me? I hate you!" I stood at my car and shook my head at him.

By this time, Grace and Simon came running out of their house.

"What is going on? What's wrong?" Simon ran over to me.

"Ask him." I sobbed.

I climbed in my car and peeled out of the driveway as fast as I could.

CHAPTER 31

*S*haun

"What happened?" Simon looked at me with anger in his eyes.

"Stay out of it, Simon," I said as I began to walk away.

"The hell I will." He grabbed my arm and spun me around. "What the hell did you do to her!" His hands grabbed my shirt, and his face was mere inches from mine.

"Simon, stop," Grace said.

"I told you to stay out of it!" I shouted in his face. "This is between her and me!"

"That's where you're wrong, buddy. What affects her affects all of us."

"Simon, let him go," Grace said as she broke his grip from me and stood between us.

"What the hell is going on out here?" Stefan asked as he ran over.

"Something happened between him and Jenni. She peeled out of the driveway crying her eyes out."

"Well, violence isn't going to solve anything, bro."

"It will if he laid a hand on her in any way."

"I didn't! I would never hurt her."

"Well, it looks to me like you already did!" Simon shouted.

"Just do me a favor and leave me the hell alone." I shook my head, walked back into the house, and locked the door.

Walking over to the island, I grabbed all the pictures, took them to my office, and ran them through the shredder. How could I have been so careless to leave that drawer unlocked? Looking over at my desk, I noticed a piece of paper with Jenni's writing. That must have been the reason she was in here. She needed a piece of paper to write whatever this was down.

Walking over to my bar, I picked up the bottle of scotch that was pretty much empty and threw it at the wall as it shattered into pieces. I sat down on the couch and placed my face in my hands as tears streamed from my eyes. My entire life had just blown up, and I didn't know what to do. Picking up my phone, I called Adam.

"Hey, Shaun."

"I need you to come to the house."

"Sure. Is everything okay?"

"No. Jenni found out. Bring a couple of bottles of scotch with you."

"Shit. I'm on my way."

~

*J*enni

The second I got home, I ran to my bedroom and threw myself on the bed. My face was soaked from all the tears, and my heart ached so bad I felt like I was dying. Curling up into a ball, a thousand emotions flowed through me. The hurt was unbearable, and I wasn't sure I was ever going to get through it. I heard the door open, and I knew it was Julia, for she was the only one who had a key. As much as I loved my sister and needed her, now wasn't the time.

"What happened?" she ran over to the bed and wrapped her arms around me.

Grace walked over to the other side, climbed next to me, and brought my head to her lap.

"We're here for you. If you don't want to talk, that's fine," she said as she stroked my hair.

"I hate him so much," I cried.

"What did he do?" Julia asked. "You need to tell us, sis."

I took in a deep breath and sat up. Scooting over, Julia climbed on the bed next to me and handed me a tissue.

"If I tell you, you both have to promise me you won't say a word to anyone. Not Sam, not Simon, no one."

"We promise," Julia said.

"You know you can trust us," Grace spoke.

"Pinky swear." I held up my pinky finger.

Julia and Grace wrapped their pinky fingers around mine.

"We promise. Whatever you tell us stays in this room," Julia said.

I blew my nose and took in a deep breath.

"Shaun is Henry's son."

"What?!" Julia exclaimed.

"Wait, if he's Henry's son, then that means the boys are his brothers," Grace spoke.

I nodded my head.

"I found a letter his mother wrote before she passed telling him everything about Henry. When he came home, I confronted him, and he told me it was true. That's not the worst part. I also found file folders with pictures of Henry, the boys, and me. He was using me all this time to get to them."

"Oh my God," Grace said. "I should have let Simon beat the shit out of him."

"I have no words right now," Julia reached over and grabbed my hand.

"What exactly did the letter say?" Graced asked.

"Just that she had lied to him, and Henry was his father. She said now that she was gone, he didn't have to be alone. She went on to say how Henry was the love of her life, and the day she was going to tell him she was pregnant, he came over and broke it off with her because he'd just found out that Barb was carrying the four boys, and he'd asked her to marry him."

"Did Shaun's mother tell Henry she was pregnant?"

"No. But she did tell someone else."

"Who?" Julia asked.

"Barb. Apparently, Shaun's mother met her in a coffee shop and told her all about the affair."

"My mother-in-law knew about him all this time and kept it a secret from Henry?"

"Shit is really going to hit the fan when he finds out about this," Grace said.

"It hurts so bad," I cried. "I just want the pain to stop."

"I know, sweetie." Julia pulled me into her. "And it will in time."

"No. No amount of time will heal this pain. I loved him so much. He told me that he loved me today and that I was the most important person in his life. But I'm sure he was just saying that because I found out. He's scared I'm going to tell the boys."

"Are you going to?" Grace asked.

"I told him he better or I will. How am I going to get through this? My company, the studio. It was all in his plan. He didn't buy me that studio because he believed in me and my designs. He did it because he was using me." I sobbed.

Julia's phone kept going off, and she finally got up and grabbed it from her purse.

"It's Sam. I have to feed the girls. I'll be back later."

"No, Julia. You have two babies at home who need you. I'll be okay."

"I'm going to stay with her tonight," Grace said.

"I feel horrible that I have to leave you like this."

"Don't. It's okay."

She kissed the top of my head. "I'll call you later. Thanks, Grace, for being here for her."

CHAPTER 32

*S*haun

"How the hell did she find out?" Adam asked as he poured me a glass of scotch.

"She found the letter and the files in my office. You should have seen her, Adam. She was distraught and heartbroken. She couldn't even bring herself to listen to me."

"Do you blame her, Shaun? I warned you this would happen."

"She told me I better tell my brothers, or she will."

"Do you think she actually would?"

"Yes. But before I do, I need to talk to her."

"Good luck with that. I'm not sure she'll ever talk to you again. Do you want my advice? You need to tell your brothers and your father who you are before this blows up even more. Jenni is just the tip of the iceberg. Then brace yourself for the fallout with them."

"I know." I threw back my drink and poured myself another glass.

Adam and I talked some more, and then he left. He had to catch an early flight back to New York in the morning.

Picking up my phone, I tried to call Jenni, and it went straight to voicemail.

"Jenni, I know you don't want to talk to me, but I love you, and I need you. Trust me when I say that I fell for you the moment you walked into the restaurant, and we had dinner together. I'm sorry for not being honest with you from the start. I'm an asshole, and I'm going to tell my brothers everything before I tell Henry that I'm his son. I love you so much. Please call me."

I threw my phone down, picked up the scotch, and started drinking it straight from the bottle.

~

*J*enni
    I was sitting in a hot bubbly tub when my phone rang. Grace showed me that Shaun was calling, and I pushed her hand away.

"Block his number for me. I'm never talking to him again."

"He left a voicemail."

"I don't care. Delete it."

"I know you're hurting. I've been there with Simon. You know that because you were there for me when I had nobody else. You were there for all the girls after the guys hurt them the way Shaun hurt you. We understand your pain, Jen."

"No wonder he hurt me so badly. He has the Kind blood running through his veins," I said.

"True. But that also could be a good thing too."

"How can you say that?" I furrowed my brows at her.

"The guys are all amazing men. Sure, they had their issues at first, but look at them now. Shaun has that blood in him too."

"Are you actually defending him?"

163

"Absolutely not." She shook her head. "But sometimes you have to put yourself in someone else's shoes to see things clearly."

"He had set it up so he met you and Simon at that bar in the hotel. He lied about what he was doing there! And what about the plane back to California? You think it was just a coincidence that he happened to be in the seat right across from the two of you?"

"No. I'm sure he orchestrated that as well. What I'm saying is he found out about an entire family he never knew he had. That has to be hard on a person. Something like that can really mess with your head. His mother lied to him his entire life about his father."

"Yeah, and that's where he gets his lies from. It was so easy for him to spew one lie after another."

"You don't know that for sure, Jen. You don't know what he was struggling with eternally."

She pressed the button on my phone, and Shaun's message started to play.

"Turn it off, Grace."

"No. You need to listen to it. You don't have to forgive him, but you have to listen."

As I sat there and listened, tears streamed down my face. The insufferable pain I felt worsened, and I didn't think that was possible. Once the message ended, Grace set down my phone and rubbed my back.

"Now, you can start to heal from all this. If you want, I'll block his number."

I nodded my head as my arms around my legs tightened.

"Done. Simon is on his way over. I couldn't stop him. You know how he is. And he's worried about you."

"Great." I shook my head.

"I'm going to go out there while you get out of the tub.

Your skin is already starting to prune." She gave me a small smile.

I climbed out of the tub, dried off, and grabbed my robe that hung on the hook on the back of the door. When I walked into the living room, I saw Simon sitting on the couch. The moment he looked at me, I started sobbing. He got up, walked over to me, and tightly wrapped his arms around me.

"It's okay. Let it all out." He walked me over to the couch. "Do you want to talk about it?"

I shook my head.

He held me until I couldn't cry anymore. Grace walked over and handed me a box of tissues. Grabbing one, I blew my nose and asked Grace if she could get me some Tylenol. My head was pounding, and I couldn't take it anymore.

"I hate seeing you like this," Simon said as I rested my head on his shoulder. "Let me take care of him."

"Leave him alone."

"Are you sure? I mean, between Grace and me, we can rough him up bad. Grace is great at breaking limbs."

"Thanks a lot, babe."

I couldn't help but let out a light laugh.

"Maybe a few days in the hospital will make him think twice about ever hurting you again."

"Stop. Just leave him alone."

"Okay. I will, for now. But you just give me the word, and I'll smash his face in."

"Simon, you are not helping," Grace said.

He stayed for a while longer, and after he left, Grace and I sat on the couch and shared two pints of Ben and Jerry's ice cream and a bottle of wine.

CHAPTER 33

*S*haun

    A couple of days had passed, and I hadn't seen or heard from her. But did I really expect to? I hadn't left the house, not even to go sit out on the patio for the risk of seeing my brothers. I needed to tell them, and it needed to be tonight.

Picking up my phone, I sent a group message.

"Can you all come to my house tonight around seven? There's something I need to tell you. Just come in through the sliding door."

All four of them responded that they'd be here. I tried to send a text message to Jenni, but it wouldn't go through. She'd blocked me like I knew she would. I cleaned up the house, sat down on the couch with my guitar, and strummed the chords to *Raining in Paris*.

As I paced around the living room, I thought about what Jenni had said about me thinking I was God. I was a billionaire who could go anywhere and do anything I wanted. My first thought was to pack up and leave the country for a couple of months and then go back to New York and live my life. But I started this war, and I needed to finish it right here in California. But after I tell my brothers and my father who I am, I would do just that. Jenni hated me and would probably never speak to me again, and the same would go for my brothers. Staying in this house would be too damn hard because I'd be seeing her over at Simon's or Sam's, and I couldn't deal with that knowing she hated me and would never be a part of my life again.

It was five minutes after seven when my brothers stepped through the sliding door and into my living room. I was already seated on the couch with a bottle of scotch and four filled glasses for them sitting on the coffee table.

"We're here," Simon spoke in an angry tone.

"Thanks for coming. Grab a glass of scotch and sit down."

"Maybe we don't want to sit. We aren't planning on staying," Simon spoke. "So just tell us whatever it is you have to say, and then we're out of here."

"Trust me when I tell you that you'll want to be sitting for this."

All four of them took a seat while I stood up and took the letter from my mother out of my pocket.

"This is a letter that my mother wrote and left explicit instructions that if and when she passed away, it was to be given to me." I handed it to Simon. "Can you just go ahead and read it out loud?"

"My dearest Shaun,

If you're reading this, that means you have already laid me to rest in the ground. I know I wasn't always the perfect mother, but I tried. Growing up without a father was hard on you, and I know your Uncle Nate attempted to fill those shoes when he came back to New York, even though he had issues of his own.

There are things I'd never told you. I suppose I took the coward's way out by telling you this when I'm dead and buried. But since your uncle is gone, and I'm gone, I don't want you to be alone in the world. I didn't lie to you when I told you that your father was a stranger I'd met in a bar. I just didn't tell you the whole truth. He was a stranger, and we did meet in a bar one night. I was with my girlfriends, and he walked over to me with the most beautiful smile I'd ever seen."

"Jesus Christ, what does this have to do with anything?" Simon spoke with irritation.

"Give it to me," Sam said as he took it from Simon's hand and continued reading.

"We left the bar together and went to a diner where we talked until two a.m. We started seeing each other after that night for a few months. I knew he was in a relationship with another woman, but I didn't care. He had stolen my heart in so many ways. He told me I was his soulmate and that he could never love another woman the way he loved me, and he was planning on breaking it off with the other woman. The best thing that had ever happened to me was finding out I was pregnant with you. The night I was to tell him about you, he had come over to tell me that we couldn't see each other anymore because the woman he was with was pregnant, and she was" — He looked up at me.

"What? She was what? Come on, Sam. Finish reading it," Stefan said.

"Carrying quadruplets. He said he needed to do the right thing, so he asked her to marry him. I was distraught and so angry. I'd felt like my heart had been ripped into a million tiny pieces, and I hated him for that. I begged him to stay with me. He told me he couldn't, and as soon as he was married, he was moving to California to start his own company. I figured if he could hurt the person he claimed so much to love, he would hurt you one day as well. So, I never told him I was pregnant. I'd kept tabs on him and his wife after they moved to California. Two months before you were born, she" — he paused and ran his hand down his face. I could see the tears swell in his eyes.

Sebastian grabbed the letter from Sam and continued reading it.

"She had her babies, and he had become the father of four boys. He was the reason I never married or was involved in a long-term relationship. I could never love anyone as I loved him. Your father's name is Henry Kind—I can't," he said as he handed the letter to Stefan.

"He lives in California and is the owner of Kind Design & Architecture. He's your blood, my darling son, as well as your four brothers. You don't need to do anything with this information, but I couldn't rest in peace until you knew the truth. You're not alone in the world, Shaun. As you're reading this, I'm sure anger and hate for me have consumed you. All I wanted to do was protect you, whether you believe me or not. Just know that I love you very much, and I will always watch over you."

I stood in the center of the room with my hands tucked tightly into my pants pockets while I stared down at the floor.

"You're our brother?" Simon asked.

"There's five of us?" Stefan's brows furrowed. "No, wait. There's six of us counting Nora."

"Does our father know about this?" Sam asked.

"No." I shook my head. "Not yet."

"Jenni found out, didn't she?" Sebastian asked.

"Yeah. Before I had the chance to tell her or all of you."

"You fucking dick!" Simon stood up, grabbed me by my shirt, and held me in place. "You knew all this time, and you never told us!" He spat in my face. "You knew the night you met Grace and me in New York?" He shook me.

"Bro, stop." Sebastian stood up.

"Fuck off, Sebastian! This is bullshit!"

"Simon," Sam stood up and placed his hand on his shoulder. "Stop. We need to talk about this like adults."

He let go of me and rubbed the back of his neck while he paced around the room.

"Fuck him and fuck Dad!" he shouted.

"You should have told us, Shaun," Stefan spoke in a calm voice.

"I was going to."

"Okay. Let's just all calm down, grab another drink, and talk this out," Sam said. "Shaun, Simon, sit down. This is serious and life-altering. Just sit down and shut up."

"So, your mother never told our dad that she was pregnant?" Sebastian asked.

"Judging by what she said in the letter, no."

"And you're one hundred percent sure he doesn't know about you?" Stefan asked.

"No. He doesn't know."

"And how can you be so sure?" Simon narrowed his eye at me.

"Because. The only other person in the world that knows never told him."

"Who else knows?" Sam's brows furrowed.

I looked down for a moment.

"Who else knows, Shaun?" Simon yelled.

I glanced over at him. "Your mother."

"What!" Simon placed his hands on his head.

CHAPTER 34

*S*haun

"The day Julia went into labor, and we were all at the hospital, your mother was waiting for me outside of the restroom. She told me she knew who I was and asked if Henry had figured it out yet. She said my mother tracked her down at a coffee shop one day and told her everything about their affair and that she was pregnant also. Your mother told me that she was afraid that if our father knew about me, he would run back to my mother, and she couldn't have that."

"Jesus Christ." Sebastian shook his head. "How could she have kept that a secret from him all these years?"

"She was pregnant with us and scared. That's how," Stefan said.

"What are your intentions with us?" Sam asked.

"Nothing. I'm going to admit that I hated you when I first found out about the four of you. I hated you for merely existing because if it weren't for you, I would have had a father in my life. But I also hated you because you got to grow up with him in yours."

"Yeah. Well, I, for one, can tell you that it wasn't all unicorns and rainbows," Stefan said.

"He probably would have done the same thing to your mother as he did to ours. He did it to the other women he was married to," Sebastian said. "Don't think he was the father of the year because he wasn't. He was barely there for us."

"And when he was, it was because it suited him," Simon said.

"We don't want you to think that we grew up in a happy and stable environment because we didn't," Sam spoke. "Our childhood was probably just as fucked up as yours was."

"All I ever wanted was a father. Someone who would teach me how to throw a baseball, shoot hoops—"

"Unfortunately, your mom picked the wrong guy to get knocked up by," Stefan said, and Sebastian reached over and slapped him across the back of his head.

"What? It's the damn truth, bro, and you know it."

"What about Jenni?" Simon asked. "Were you using her to get to us?"

I sat there and slowly nodded my head. "At first, that was my plan, but she is the most amazing woman I've ever met in my life, and I fell in love with her so fast. Now that I've lost her, I don't know what I'm going to do."

"You're going to go back to New York, and you're going to forget about her and us. Do you understand me?" Simon shouted as he stood up. "I will never consider you my brother. Blood or not. I'm out of here."

"Simon, wait!" Sam said.

"Let him go, Sam. I don't blame him. In fact, the three of you can go too. I know this is a lot to take in. Trust me. I was just as angry when I first found out."

"When do you plan on telling our father?" Stefan asked.

"I don't know. Maybe Simon is right. I should just go back to New York and never come back here again."

"You can't run from the truth, Shaun," Sam said. "Simon will come around. He always does. As for Jenni, I'm not so sure. This is a lot of information to take in, and I'm sure my brothers agree."

"It sure is," Sebastian said.

"I knew it." Stefan pointed to Sam and Sebastian. "I told you he was cheating on Mom back then. I told you, and I was right! Damn, I love when I'm right." He grinned.

"Yeah. You were right." Sam rolled his eyes.

"You need to talk to our dad, Shaun," Sebastian said. "We'll help you with that, and we'll be there for you when you tell him."

"I appreciate it, but how can you after everything I've done?"

"Trust me. It's really hard."

"It's going to take time for us to get used to this. So, maybe it's best you lay low for a while," Sam spoke.

"Yeah. I know." I lowered my head.

"You're not a bad person, Shaun. You're a good man. You just went about this all wrong."

"I know I did, Sam, and I'm sorry."

"We're gonna go," Sebastian said. "We'll talk to you later." He placed his hand on my shoulder.

"Yeah. We'll talk some more once we've had time to process all of this," Stefan spoke as he walked past me.

Sam gave me a nod as he walked by, and the three of them left. After cleaning up, I headed to bed. Grabbing my phone, I pulled up the picture of Jenni that I had taken. I missed her. I let anger, hatred, and revenge get the best of me, and I wasn't sure if I could even repair the damage I had done.

The following morning, I got up at the crack of dawn and

right before the sun rose. Grabbing my coffee, I went down to the beach and nestled myself in the sand as the sun was starting to rise, giving a rosy and golden tone to the sky. It was beautiful, and I'd wished Jenni was here to see it with me. After finishing my coffee, I set the cup down in the sand and stared out at the vast blue water. As I was sitting there reflecting on all the wrongs I've done, I heard a voice from behind.

"Hi, Shaun."

Turning around, I saw Lily standing there.

"Good morning, Lily. Why are you up so early?"

"I'm an early riser," she said as she sat down next to me. "Why are you up so early?"

I let out a sigh. "I couldn't sleep."

"Do you have too much going on in your head?"

The corners of my mouth curved upward as I glanced over at her.

"I do."

"Adult stuff?"

"Yeah. Adult stuff."

"I probably shouldn't say anything. My dad always tells me that I need to learn when to keep my mouth shut."

I let out a chuckle.

"I overheard my parents talking last night. They don't think I hear them, but I do. I have excellent ears. My dad told my mom that you're his brother and that Grandpa Henry is your dad, but Grandpa doesn't know about you."

Shit. Good going, Stefan.

"Is it true? And don't feel like you have to lie to me because my mom always says she doesn't believe in lying to children and that they deserve to know the truth so they can learn to handle situations early on."

"Alex said that?"

"Yeah. She never lies to me."

"But sometimes there are adult things that children can't quite comprehend yet."

"I can. I'm smart."

"I know you are." I gave her a wink.

"So, is it true?" She cocked her head. "Are you my Uncle Shaun?"

I stared into her eyes for a moment before I answered her question.

"Yes. I am your uncle."

"That's so cool." She grinned. "Now, I have four uncles. Why didn't your mom tell Grandpa about you?"

"It's complicated, Lily. Sometimes, adults don't make the right or good decisions."

"Just like kids, right?"

"Yeah. Sometimes kids don't either."

"If Grandpa had known about you, he would have been there for you. He's always been there for me."

"I'm sure he would have been. I need you to promise me that you won't tell him that you know until after I talk with him."

"I won't. I pinky swear." She held up her little finger. "Wrap yours around mine, and it'll become our little secret."

I wrapped my pinky finger around hers.

~

*S*tefan

"Alex, come here!" I shouted as I stared out the sliding door at Shaun and Lily.

"What is it?"

"Look. Lily is down there talking to Shaun."

"So?" Her brows furrowed.

"I'm not sure that's a good idea. God knows what she's saying to him."

"Relax." Alex wrapped her arm around my waist.

"I can't. I have to go down there."

"No, you're not. Leave them alone."

"Oh my God! Is she hugging him? Why the hell is she hugging him?"

"You can ask her in a minute. Look, she's on her way up to the house."

Alex kissed my cheek and went to get Henry from his crib. I opened the sliding door as Lily approached it.

"Morning, Daddy." She smiled.

"Morning. Why were you down there talking to Shaun?"

"Why not?" Her brows furrowed. "Do you have a problem with him, Dad?" She cocked her head at me.

"No."

"Good. I like Uncle Shaun. And before you get your crazy eyes going, I overheard you and mom talking last night about him. I. HEARD. EVERYTHING."

I ran my hand down my face as I propped myself up against the island.

"Don't worry. I pinky swore I wouldn't tell Grandpa or anyone else. I gave him my word, and the Kind word is never broken, right, Dad?" Her little brow arched.

"Right." I stood there and shook my head in disbelief.

"I'm going to play my game. Can you make me some eggs and toast? Oh, and can you call Uncle Sebastian and see if he has any of those cinnamon rolls left? Thanks, Daddy." She smiled as she walked away.

Alex walked in and handed Henry over to me.

"I heard that conversation. Are you okay?" Alex's lips formed a smirk.

"What did she mean by 'crazy eyes?' What the hell?"

"You know, babe. Right before you get really mad, you get this crazy look in your eyes." She smiled.

"I most certainly do not."

"Yeah, you do."

"No, I don't!"

"See. There it is." She pointed to my eyes before reaching up and kissing my lips.

CHAPTER 35

*J*enni

I'd spent the last four days locked in my apartment and lying in bed. I told Wes and my staff that I had the flu and would be in when I felt better. I'd called Seymour Klaus to reschedule our meeting, and he was leaving the country for a month, so he said he'd call when he got back. I was certain I fucked that up, but I couldn't bring myself to leave my apartment. The more I thought about it, the angrier I became. I was broken into a million tiny pieces, but there was no way in hell I was going to let what had happened ruin my dream. So, I took in a deep breath, climbed out of bed, took a shower, and got ready for work.

"Good morning, everyone." I put on a smile for my staff. "I'm back, and we have a lot of work to catch up on."

Wes walked over and hooked his arm around me. "Welcome back. God, have I missed you. Are you feeling better?"

I glanced over at him as we walked up the stairs to my office, and the uncontrollable tears fell from my eyes.

"Oh my God. What's wrong?"

We went into my office, shut the door, and I told him everything.

"I thought I was done crying," I dried my eyes with a tissue.

"You may think that from time to time, but when you least expect it, the tears will come back. It's still so fresh, Jen. It's going to take time." He hugged me.

I was in the middle of making changes to a coat I'd designed when I heard a voice from behind.

"Can I talk to you?"

My heart started racing as I stood with my back to him.

"Now isn't a good time. I'm busy."

I heard my office door shut, and when I turned around, I saw Shaun standing there holding a round black decorative box filled with red roses from Venus ET Fleur.

"I know how much you love red roses, and I'm sorry I never bought them for you before." He held the box out to me.

"That's because our relationship was fake. Why would you buy a fake someone you're in a fake relationship with, fake flowers?"

He inhaled a sharp breath.

"It was never fake to me, Jenni."

"Right." I nodded as I took the box and set it on my desk.

"I'm not even going to ask you how you're doing because I know you're not doing well. Just like I'm not."

"You're wrong, Shaun. I'm great."

"Now, who's the one lying?" he said.

"What do you want me to say? You want me to tell you how broken I am? How the insufferable pain in my heart makes me want to stay in bed all day? And how much I hate myself that I ever trusted you in the first place?"

"Jen, I'm so sorry."

"I don't care if you're sorry. Because even if you truly are,

I will never forgive you. I made the mistake of doing that once in my lifetime, and I will never make that mistake again. Can you please leave? I have a lot of work to do."

"I'll leave for now, but this isn't over."

"The hell it isn't." I turned around and away from him.

He walked out and slammed the door. Within seconds, the door opened again, and Wes came running over.

"Are you okay?"

"Does it look like I'm okay?" I started to cry.

"What beautiful flowers. I love those! They last a whole year. Did you know that?"

I glared at him, walked over to my desk, grabbed the box, and threw it in the garbage.

"OMG! NO!" he shouted as he walked over and grabbed the box. "Jen, these are fifteen-hundred-dollar roses! No. No. No."

"I don't care if they cost fifteen thousand dollars. Get them the fuck out of here." I snapped.

"Okay. Calm down. I'll get these stunning roses out of your sight."

⁓

*S*am
"Sorry, I'm late. My meeting ran longer than I thought it would," I said as I sat down with my brothers at our family table.

"I don't know why we're even here. Nothing is going to change my mind about him," Simon said.

"He's our brother, Simon."

"The hell he is."

"Okay. He lied to all of us. We've all lied," Stefan said.

"Yeah, but this is a little different, bro," Sebastian spoke.

"The point is, he's our father's son and our brother. I

don't like the things he did, but can you really blame him?" I asked.

"Are you fucking serious?!" Simon shouted.

"Bro, not in my restaurant," Sebastian said.

"You have every right to be angry. We all do. But you're a bit extreme. Is it the fact that he hurt Jenni or that he's a reminder of what we already know about Dad?" I asked Simon.

"He hurt Jenni. He used her to get to us!"

"Bro, be honest. This is us," Stefan said. "Yeah, I'm pissed how he hurt Jenni, but I don't believe that was his intention. I saw the way he looked at her. It's the same look we get when we stare at our women. You can't fake that."

"Shut the fuck up, Stefan," Simon said as he slammed back his drink.

"Mom is the one we should be pissed at. She knew all these years about him, and she never told Dad. Shaun acted the way he did because of Dad. He was seeing another woman while he was seeing Mom. No wonder they were always fighting. I couldn't imagine keeping a secret like that for thirty-three years."

"Put yourself in his shoes," I said. "The fact of the matter is he's our brother, and he has the same blood running through his veins that we do. Our father made him, and there's nothing we can do to change that. It's not his fault, and you need to accept that, bro." I pointed at Simon.

"I agree. He did some shady shit, and he lied. Who hasn't? He made a mistake, and it's not like all of us haven't made our fair share in our lifetime," Sebastian said.

"And it's not like he's here to get money from us or anything. The guy is fucking worth fifteen billion dollars," Stefan said. "Fifteen billion that he made on his own. He's a genius, and to be honest, I'm kind of jealous."

"Yeah. No shit." Sebastian shook his head.

"If there's one thing that our beautiful women have taught us, it's forgiveness. Just imagine where we'd be right now and how different our lives would be if they didn't forgive us for what we'd done. Shaun is a Kind, and we Kind men protect one another and our families," I said.

Simon got up from the table and walked out of the restaurant.

"He'll come around," I spoke.

"I hope so," Stefan said.

My phone rang, and when I pulled it from my pocket, I saw Celeste was calling.

"Hello."

"Sam, are you with your brothers?"

"Yeah. We're at the restaurant. Why?"

"Your father is in the hospital."

"What? Why?"

"He's been ill for a while, and he never told anyone. I think you boys need to get down here. He's going to be pissed, but I don't care."

"We're on our way, Celeste."

"What's wrong?" Sebastian asked.

"Dad is in the hospital. We have to go, now. Stefan, text Simon and tell him to meet us there."

"I'm on it."

CHAPTER 36

$\mathcal{S}$haun

I sat out on the patio with a bottle of scotch, a glass, and my guitar. I had hoped talking to Jenni would have gone better. But what did I expect? It was clear she truly hated me, and I didn't know how to handle it. I just needed to close the house and go back to New York to try and get over her.

As I was strumming my guitar, Simon stepped out on his patio and looked at me.

"You know I really hate that you removed that wall," he shouted.

"Yeah. I'm sorry about that. I'll have the guys come out and put another one back up."

He went inside his house, and I continued to play my guitar. The next thing I knew, he walked over with a glass in his hand.

"You don't mind, right?" He grabbed the bottle of scotch off the table.

"No. Help yourself."

He poured himself a glass and sat down.

"Our dad is in the hospital."

"What? Why?" My brows furrowed.

"The doctors aren't sure what's wrong with him yet. They're still running tests. Apparently, he hasn't been well, and he's been hiding it from everyone."

"I'm not surprised considering how he was at his birthday party."

"What are you talking about?" Simon asked.

"I noticed he was having shortness of breath."

"And you didn't say anything?" His voice raised.

"I said something to Stefan about it, and he said he's fine."

"You noticed, and none of us did." He shook his head.

"I'm sure he's going to be fine, Simon."

"Yeah. Hopefully. Grace told me she talked to Jenni today. She said you went to see her at the studio."

"Yeah. What a disaster that was." I brought my glass up to my mouth. "She told me she will never forgive me and that she's made that mistake once in her lifetime, and she won't do it again."

Simon let out a light chuckle.

"Sounds like Jenni. Sorry, man. I don't mean to laugh. I know you're hurting."

"I don't think you do, Simon."

"Yeah. I do. When Grace left and went back to Washington, I was in so much pain. It was my fault because I couldn't admit how I felt about her. She was staying at my place while we were working on a case, and when the case was over, I offered to help her find a place of her own. And I told her not to stay in California just for me."

"Ouch."

"Yeah. It wasn't pretty. And Sam." He shook his head. "He told Julia he was choosing money over her and that he didn't give a damn about her dreams. Then he told her she was nothing but his personal assistant and a woman he fucked."

"Come on. No, he didn't!" My eyes widened.

"Yep. He sure did, and Sebastian and Stefan weren't any better with Emilia and Alex. Compliments of our daddy issues and what we witnessed growing up between our parents. You know what, Shaun? You're just as fucked up, compliments of your daddy issues, aka, Henry Kind. Welcome to the family." He held up his glass to me.

"I'm not sure if I should thank you or not." I smirked as I tapped my glass against his.

"Anyway, if Julia, Emilia, Alex, and Grace, could forgive us, Jenni will forgive you too. It might take a long time, but she eventually will. You just have to give her space and time."

"Thanks, Simon. Listen, I am truly sorry, and I don't expect you to forgive me."

"It's going to take some time. Anyway, I don't think it's a good time to have a talk with our father about who you are. I think you need to wait until he's on the mend."

"I agree, and I won't. Not until he's better."

"You two playing nice in the sandbox?" Sam smiled as he and Stefan walked over.

"He hit me in the head with a shovel." Simon smirked.

"Only because you threw sand in my eyes." I grinned.

"Where's Sebastian?" Simon asked.

"Still at the restaurant. He'll be home soon," Stefan spoke.

"How are the girls, Sam?" I asked.

"Your nieces are a handful but absolutely worth it." He smiled.

"Dude, you must be so overwhelmed," Stefan said as he sat down next to me.

"What do you mean?"

"You grew up an only child to a single parent. Now, out of nowhere, you have a father, a stepmother, four brothers, a baby sister, two sisters-in-law, another sister-in-law on the way, three nieces, and a nephew. Did I forget anyone?"

"Damn. I'm feeling overwhelmed," Simon said, and we all laughed.

"Since you're our brother, we have some brotherly rules we need to go over with you," Sam said.

"Brotherly rules?"

"No time of the day or night is off-limits. If you need us or we need you, we drop whatever we're doing. We have a group chat the four of us use that you'll be included in. Our houses are yours, and yours is ours. You'll be expected to surf with us every week. We have family dinners at the restaurant once a week you must attend. And as you know, we get together on the weekends and drink and play the guitar."

"You up for all that?" Simon asked.

The corners of my mouth curved upward. "Yeah, I'm up for it."

"What's going on over here?" Sebastian walked over with his guitar and sat down.

"We're just filling our brother in on our rules," Sam said.

"Oh yeah?" Sebastian looked at me. "We have one more. You have to know how to play Sweet Home Alabama. If you can do that, you're in."

"You mean like this?" I started strumming the song.

"YOU. ARE. THE. MAN!" Stefan grinned as he pointed at me.

Sebastian played with me, and the five of us sat there and sang the lyrics together.

As much fun as I had with my brothers, an insufferable pain still resided inside me over Jenni. I would get her back one way or another because I was Shaun Sterling, and I always get what I want.

CHAPTER 37

ONE WEEK LATER

*J*enni

I was at the studio going over fabric samples with Rena, one of my designers, when the studio door opened. When I turned around, I saw Shaun step in and two guys behind him carrying in a large desk.

"It's going right up here," he said as he walked up the stairs.

"What is going on?" I dropped the fabric samples and tried to get past the two men with the desk.

The door opened again, so I turned around and saw more men bringing in large boxes.

"What is in those boxes?" I stopped the one man.

"Computer equipment," he said.

"No. No. No." I shook my head. "You turn yourself around and put those boxes back in your truck."

"Lady, come on."

"Did you hear what I just said?" I pointed to the door.

"Excuse me? What do you think you're doing?" Shaun asked as he walked over to me.

"The question is, what do you think you're doing?" I scowled at him.

"Take those up," he said to the men. "I'm setting up my office."

"You're what?" I shouted as I narrowed my eye at him.

"I need an office, and this is my building."

"You have your home office! And there are a million buildings for lease/sale in Los Angeles. Go find one!"

"I like this location." The corners of his mouth curved upward. "Plus, it's close to my house, and I won't have to fight traffic every day."

"You cannot do this, Shaun."

"Sure, I can. Like I said, I own the building. Now, if you'll excuse me, I have an office to set up." He smiled as he turned and headed back up the stairs.

I stood there in the middle of the first floor of my studio with such anger that I couldn't see straight.

"Oh my." Wes smiled as he walked over and placed his hand on my shoulder. "This is going to be very interesting."

I shot him a look, stomped up the stairs, and went into my office. Opening my laptop, I Facetimed Julia.

"Hey, you." She smiled as she held Lena in her arms.

"Can you believe he's putting an office in my studio? Can you believe it?"

"Slow down, sis. What are you talking about?"

"Shaun!"

"Well, it is his building."

"Wow. Really, Julia?"

"Jen, there's nothing you can do if he wants an office there. You're just going to have to deal with it. Stay away from him."

"Stay away from him? I'm sitting here staring at him from across the hall! His desk faces mine!"

"Hello, darling." My mother's face appeared on the screen.

"Mom. I didn't know you were over there."

"I'm helping Julia with the girls. I heard everything you said, and there's no use getting yourself all worked up over something you can't control. Just make the best of the situation."

"Ugh. I have to go." I ended the call.

Glancing over at his office, he stood there with his hands tucked into his pants pockets, watching the men as they unboxed and hooked up his computers.

"This isn't happening," I whispered as I placed my hand on my forehead.

The pain in my heart was still unbearable, and the only thing that got me through the days was being able to come here and keep busy enough to keep my mind off him. How was I supposed to get over him when I saw him every day? It was bad enough that every night when my head hit the pillow, the tears would fall. Damn these glass walls. Picking up my phone, I sent Wes a text message.

"Get up here!"

"Yes, your highness?" He grinned when he stepped inside.

"I need you to measure this wall." I pointed to the wall that faced Shaun's office.

"Why?"

"Because I need to know how much fabric to cut."

"You're going to cover this glass with fabric?" His brow arched.

"You bet I am. Now get measuring while I go get it."

I stomped out of my office, went downstairs, grabbed a bolt of black fabric and the masking tape.

"This is how much you need." Wes handed me a piece of paper.

"Good, let's get cutting."

I laid the bolt of fabric on the floor and unrolled it.

"Umm, there isn't enough here," Wes said.

"I can see that!" I spoke with irritation. "Fuck!" I got up from the floor, and when I stood back and looked at the wall made of glass, I saw Shaun standing in his office staring at me. "I have an idea. Let's just cut enough to cover this part right here."

"You mean the direct view from his desk to yours?"

"Yes. That's exactly what I mean."

Wes cut the fabric, and I hung it.

"There." I smiled.

"Feel better?" he asked as we stood there with our arms folded.

"Actually, I do. Just because his brothers forgave him, I don't."

Wes let out a sigh as he hooked his arm around me. "I read a quote once that really stuck with me when I was going through a hard time."

"What quote was that?" I asked him.

"It takes a strong person to say sorry and an even stronger person to forgive."

"Then I guess I'm not that strong."

"But darling, you are. You just refuse to be." He kissed my cheek and walked out of my office.

"Hey," Shaun popped his head into my office. "Nice job." He pointed to the fabric I'd hung up.

"Good. I'm glad you like it. And just so you know, you can't be coming in here whenever you feel like it. I'm very busy."

"I know how busy you are. Family dinner is at the restaurant tonight. Are you going?"

"No. I'm not going. In fact, I'm never going again!"

"Okay." He nodded his head. "Your loss. You'll be missing out on great food."

"I don't care. I'd rather starve to death than have dinner with you."

"Ouch." The corners of his mouth curved upward. "I do believe there will be cake there for dessert." He gave me a wink and turned and walked away.

My legs involuntarily tightened, and I swallowed hard at the cake memory embedded in my mind.

CHAPTER 38

*S*haun
    We had found out that Henry was anemic due to a gastrointestinal bleed he ignored. He was put on medication and had to go for iron infusions once a week for the next three weeks. Now that he was home and feeling better, my brothers told me it was time I talked to him. I had wished I had Jenni to be by my side when I revealed who I was. But she spent so much time hating me that she'd probably spit in my face and tell me to go to hell even if I asked her.

"We can't ignore the fact that Mom knew about him," Sebastian said as we all gathered around the firepit at his house.

"I agree," Sam spoke. "We need to have a talk with her and tell her that we know."

"And we need to do it before Shaun talks to Dad," Simon said.

"I just sent her a text message saying we're coming over tomorrow morning for breakfast and that Sebastian is supplying it." Stefan grinned.

"Come on, douchebag! Seriously? We'll just invite her to the restaurant."

"Not a good idea," Sam spoke. "If we meet at her house, she can't just up and leave. If she's at the restaurant, she will."

"I guess," Sebastian said.

"How is it going at the office with Jenni?" Simon smirked.

"Aside from the fact that she put up black fabric over a part of the glass so I can't see her, or the fact that she said she'd rather starve to death than have dinner with me, I'd say things are going quite well." I took a sip of my drink.

All four of them chuckled.

"Ah, that's why she hasn't been at family dinner," Simon said. "I sent her a text message asking her where the hell she's been, and she said she's been busy."

~

Sebastian

"This is such a nice surprise," our mother spoke as we all sat around the table having breakfast. "Thank you, darling, for all this delicious food." She reached over and placed her hand on my cheek.

"You're welcome, Mom." I looked at my brothers.

"Mom, we didn't just come here for breakfast. We came here to talk to you," Sam spoke.

"What about?"

"Well—We—" He cleared his throat.

"Oh, for fuck's sake. We know Shaun is Dad's son and our brother!" Simon pointed at her. "And we also know that you knew all this time and never told anyone."

"Bro," Stefan said, and I let out a sigh.

She sat there and stared at each of us and didn't say a word.

"Come on, Mom. At least try to defend yourself," Simon

193

said.

"Yes, I did know."

"How could you keep the fact that we had another brother a secret from us?" I asked her.

"I had no choice!" She slammed her hands down on the table. "I was pregnant with the four of you.! She told me the things he'd said to her. Things he never said to me. If I would have told him about the baby, he would have left me for her. How the hell was I supposed to take care of four babies all by myself? I was young, and I was scared out of my mind!"

"You didn't know that for sure, Mom," Sam spoke.

"You let an innocent child grow up without a father," Stefan said.

"You four were more important. I did it for you. I lived in an unhappy marriage for five years for the four of you! Not for me."

"This is crazy," I said. "And just so you know, we don't appreciate you threatening Shaun the way you did."

"We expected something like that from Dad, but not you." Simon slowly shook his head.

"The four of you are finally happy and settled. I wasn't about to let a total stranger ruin that for you."

"Just so you know, Mother," Sam stood up from his chair. "We happen to like Shaun a lot, and we welcome him into our family. He's our brother, our blood. The four of us do not turn our backs on one of our own. You know that. Let's go."

"And for the record," Stefan said. "He will be at every holiday, family functions, dinners, and parties. So, you need to make things right with him."

"You do not tell me what to do, Stefan!" she shouted.

"You know what, Mom? Do the right thing for once in your life," Simon said, and the four of us walked out of the dining room and out the door.

"Jesus. This family." I shook my head.

"Alex texted me, and she just picked up Celeste and Nora to go shopping, so Dad is home alone," Stefan said.

"I'll text Shaun and tell him to head over there," Simon spoke as he pulled out his phone.

"One parent down and one more to go. Fuck!" Sam said. "There better not be any more illegitimate Kind children running around in the world."

~

*S*haun

    My phone pinged with a text message from Simon.

"Dad is home alone now, so you can head over there. We just left our mother's house, and we should be there in about twenty minutes."

"I'll head there now."

I took in a deep breath, slipped on my shoes, and walked down to Henry's. I knocked on the front door, and when he didn't answer, I went around the back and saw him sitting on the patio.

"Hey." I walked over with my hands tucked into my pants pockets. "I wanted to stop by to see how you're feeling?"

"Better. Thank you." He stared at me. "Sit down for a minute."

I took the seat in the lounger across from where he sat.

"Were you ever going to say anything, son?"

I stared into his eyes as my heart rate started to pick up.

"Eventually."

"It's only noon, but that doesn't stop men like us from having a drink. Come inside."

I swallowed the lump in my throat as I followed him into the house. He walked over to his bar cart in the living room, poured us each a glass of scotch, and handed it to me. The sliding door opened, and my four brothers walked in.

"Ah, the cavalry has arrived. If you want a drink, you know where the scotch is."

"Dad?" Sam furrowed his brows.

"He knows," I said.

"You told him already?" Stefan asked.

"No. He already knew."

"That's right, boys. Your father already knew about his other son. I had been waiting for your brother to come forth with the truth. Do the four of you remember that morning on the beach when I was sitting in the sand and watching you surf?"

"Yeah. We remember," Simon said.

"I had found out that morning. When my friend called to tell me that Louise had passed, he also told me that she had a son in his early thirties, and he looked a lot like me in my younger years. I didn't believe it at first because she would have told me she was pregnant. I figured maybe she'd met someone shortly after we stopped seeing each other. Then the letter came."

"What letter?" I furrowed my brows at him.

"The letter that her lawyer sent to me a couple of weeks after she died. I believe you also got a similar letter."

"I did."

"So, let me get this straight," Simon said. "You knew all those months ago that you had another son, and you never said anything or bothered to find him?"

"I knew he'd come to me, and with everything going on with Celeste and the pregnancy, I couldn't think about anything else. I'd been waiting for this moment since that damn letter arrived. I'm sorry, Shaun. If I would have known she was pregnant—"

CHAPTER 39

*S*haun

"You would have what, Henry? Left Barb to be with her? I don't think so. Paying child support for four kids is a hell of a lot more expensive. You ruined her!" I stood up and pointed at him.

"He has a knack for ruining people," Simon said.

"Bro, shush," Stefan said.

"What do you want me to say? I loved your mother very deeply, and it killed me to have to walk away from her, but I didn't have a choice. I did the right thing by marrying the boy's mother."

"Speaking of Barb, she knew the whole time about me."

"What?" His eye narrowed.

"My mother confronted her right before you left New York. She told her all about the affair and how she was pregnant with me."

"My God." He brought his hand up and rubbed the back of his neck. "Are you serious?"

"Yeah, Dad. The four of us came here straight from

Mom's house. We confronted her. She's kept this secret for thirty-three years," Sam said.

"If you knew who I was the night I met you at Sebastian's house, why the hell didn't you say anything?"

"Because we had just brought home your baby sister from the NICU, where she had just spent the first month of her life. Besides, I needed to figure out how to prepare Celeste and your brothers for the news. I needed to see how the five of you got along first. So, I watched from a distance."

"Wow, Dad. Again, no father of the year award for you," Simon said.

"For fuck's sake. Be quiet, Simon," Henry spewed.

"No, Dad!" Simon shouted. "I will not be quiet! You knew and didn't say a word to him or us! Have you even bothered to tell Celeste yet?"

"No. I was waiting until after Shaun and I talked."

"More secrets. Just like when we were growing up," Sebastian said.

"I'm sorry. I didn't know how to tell you boys because I didn't want you to be disappointed in me."

"Please. We've been since you and Mom got divorced," Stefan said. "Nothing new there."

"I want the four of you to leave so Shaun and I can talk in private."

"Nah. We told our brother we'd have his back. We're staying," Simon said.

"Fine. Stay then. Shaun, I'm sorry. If I could go back in time and make things right, I would. But I can't, and this situation is what it is, so we have to try and make the best of it."

"What did my mother say in her letter to you?"

"I'll go get it so you can read it. I'll be right back." He walked up the stairs.

"You guys don't have to stay. I've got this."

"As we told you before, we always have each other's backs, and we're not going to leave you alone with him." Sam placed his hand on my shoulder.

As soon as Henry walked back into the living room, he handed me the letter, and I gave him mine. Sitting down on the couch, I read it.

Henry,

If you're reading this, that means I've passed on. I wanted to let you know that you have a beautiful son named Shaun. After you left and moved away to California, he has been the highlight of my life. He's a fine young man, and he's so intelligent. He's practically a genius. He didn't get that from my side of the family, so he inherited it from you, his father. You hurt me in ways I never got over. You were the only man I had ever loved, and having Shaun was a way to keep a part of you with me. It was hard, and we struggled. But we made it, and he turned into a fine young man. A man you'd be proud to call your son. He graduated from Yale at the top of his class, and he's the CEO of his own capital company. He plays the guitar perfectly and has the voice of an angel. He is you in so many ways, Henry. I wish I had told you about him many years ago, but you had hurt me so badly that I couldn't risk you being a part of his life and hurting him one day as well. Take care, Henry, and try to get to know our son.

Love,

Louise.

Tears swelled in my eyes as I read the letter.

"You okay, bro?" Simon asked as he patted my shoulder.

"Yeah. I'm fine. She cared more about going out and bringing men home for the night than staying home and taking care of me."

"Had I known, I would have taken you from her and brought you here with us."

"That's easy for you to say now." I stood up from the couch. "I'm going to go."

"Son, wait. I am proud of you for everything you've accomplished. Just like I'm proud of my other sons and what they've accomplished. Give me a chance to be your father. I'm going to tell Celeste the minute she gets back from shopping. Like I've always told my boys, all damage can be repaired. It just depends on how badly you want to fix it. And I want to fix this."

"I don't know, Henry. Let's just see how things go." As I opened the sliding door, he called my name.

"Shaun?"

I turned around and looked at him.

"Clever move taking those millions from me." The corners of his mouth curved upward as he gave me a wink.

"Millions? What millions?" Stefan asked.

"You'll get your millions back." I walked out the door.

I couldn't believe my mother had written Henry a letter. Was I angry he didn't confront me when we'd first met? Not really. I'd done the same thing. He watched me as I watched him. It was out in the open now, and the war I'd started had come to an end between my father and my brothers. But there was one war still going on I had to fight. The war between Jenni and me. A war I was going to win no matter what.

CHAPTER 40

*J*enni

"Yes. This is perfect, Nadia. Just tighten the waistline a tiny bit."

"Good morning, everyone." Shaun walked in. "Good morning, Jenni."

"It was until now." I shot him a look and walked up to my office.

"Come on." He followed behind me. "How long are you going treat me like this?"

I stopped before I approached my office, turned, and looked at him.

"Forever."

He let out a sigh as he went to his office, and I went to mine and shut the door. A few moments later, the door opened, and Shaun walked in.

"What are you doing?" I cocked my head at him.

"Just seeing if you've turned that frown upside down yet?" His lips formed a smirk.

I picked up the pincushion sitting on my desk and threw

it, missing him as he quickly shut the door. Sitting there, I let out a breath and placed my hand on my forehead. Suddenly, my office door opened again.

"WHAT?!" I shouted.

"Girlfriend...what the hell is your problem?" Wes asked as he stood in the doorway.

"Sorry." I stood up. "It's him!" I pointed towards Shaun's office. "He's my problem!"

He walked over and gripped my shoulders.

"You need to calm the hell down. Breathe. Come on. Breathe. In and out. Good. Feel better now?"

"Sort of."

"Don't let him get to you, Jen. I mean—I'm not even sure how you can stay mad at that hunk of a man. Seriously, woman, between his looks and that cologne he wears—" Wes fanned himself with his hand.

"Knock it off. His looks and his scent don't mean shit when he's nothing but a user and a liar."

After I sent Wes on some errands, I opened my office door and noticed Shaun wasn't in his. Walking down the stairs, I asked some of my staff if they'd seen him.

"Have you seen Shaun? Did he leave?" I prayed.

"Yeah," Nadia spoke. "He left over an hour ago."

"Good." I nodded my head. "Okay. Show me what you have."

My phone in my back pocket pinged, and when I pulled it out to see who was texting me, I noticed it was from Julia.

"*Hey, sis. I'm at Sam's office with the girls, and we were supposed to go lunch, but he got called into an emergency meeting. Please say you'll come and have lunch with us. Lena and Lorelei miss their auntie.*"

A smile crossed my face. I hadn't seen them in a few days, and I missed them.

"I'll leave the studio in a few minutes. Where do you want to meet?"

"Just come to the office, and we'll take my car and drive together."

"Okay. See you soon."

I went upstairs, grabbed my purse, and headed out the door. When I arrived, I sent Julia a text message from my car.

"I'm parked next to you, but you're not in your car."

"I had to feed Lena, and now Lorelei is starting to scream. Can you please come up and help me?"

"Yeah. Of course. I'll be right up."

As I was about to open my door and climb out, a car pulled in on the other side. Looking over, I noticed it was Shaun.

"What are you doing here?" he asked as he climbed out of his car.

"What are you doing here? Are you following me?"

"No." His brows furrowed. "If I were following you, I wouldn't park next to you. I'd stalk you from a distance. Stefan called, and he said there's a problem with one of the condos. He needed me here ASAP to go over a change. Why are you here?"

"I'm meeting Julia for lunch."

"Here?" he asked as he held the door open for me.

"No. We're driving to the restaurant together, but she needs my help with the girls."

I pressed the button to the elevator, and when the doors opened, we both stepped inside.

"I still don't understand why you're meeting her here," he spoke as the elevator started going up.

"Why do you care so much?" I snapped as I cocked my head at him.

Suddenly, the elevator jerked and came to a standstill. As both Shaun and I stumbled back, he grabbed hold of my arm.

"What the hell just happened?" I jerked my arm away from him.

"I think the elevator just got stuck," he said as he quickly pushed all the buttons to the floors.

"No. No. No." I started to panic.

"Relax. I'm sure it'll start back up in a second."

Pulling my phone from my purse, I looked at it and had no service.

"Do you have service?" I asked.

"If you don't have service, what makes you think I would?" he spoke with an attitude.

I started banging on the doors and yelling for help.

"Jenni, stop."

"Don't tell me what to do!"

He reached over and pressed the emergency call button a couple of times. Suddenly, we heard a voice in the distance.

"We're aware the elevator isn't working, and we've got someone on the way to look at it. How many people are in there?"

"Two," Shaun said.

"Just relax and try to make yourselves comfortable."

"Are you kidding me?!" I shouted. "I cannot be stuck in here. Especially with him! Plus, my sister needs my help."

"Ma'am, I understand, but—"

"No! I don't think you do, sir!"

"Someone is on their way. We'll have you out in no time. Please, just try to relax."

"UGH!"

"Jen, there's no use getting worked up. It's not going to change anything."

"Be quiet, Shaun."

I sat down, leaned up against the wall, and brought my knees to my chest. Looking up, I stared at Shaun, who stood in the corner opposite me.

"Are you okay?" he asked.

"I'm fine. Why wouldn't I be?"

"I don't know if you have panic attacks or are claustrophobic. We never talked about those things."

"I'm fine." I looked away from him.

"Henry and I talked yesterday," he said as he lowered himself to the ground.

"In all honesty, Shaun, I really don't care."

"Okay then. I'll just shut up."

"Good idea."

I glanced over at him as he sat there with his legs up and his head lowered. I was being a total bitch because of how badly he hurt me. But I knew how hard it must have been telling Henry he was his son and to have to face him and talk about his mother.

"I'm sorry. How did it go?"

He lifted his head, and our eyes met.

"He already knew."

"What?" My brows furrowed. "How?"

"My mother left him a letter as well. He's known since she passed away."

"And he didn't bother to try and get in contact with you?"

"He said he was waiting for me to come to him, and with everything going on with Celeste and the baby, he couldn't think of anything else."

"Wow." I shook my head. "He truly is an asshole."

"Yeah. You think." He let out a light laugh.

"So now what?"

"I don't know. He said he was proud of me, and he wants me to give him a chance at being my father."

"What did you say?"

"I told him we'd see how things go, and I left. Sam, Sebastian, Stefan, and Simon were there. They had a few things to say to him."

"I'm sure they did." I lowered my head.

"I wish you would have been there."

"Don't. Don't do that."

"It's the truth, Jen."

I huffed out a laugh.

CHAPTER 41

*S*haun

"I know I'm an asshole. You remind me every day, and I'm sorry. I truly am. I never meant to hurt you."

"STOP! Just stop!" she shouted as she raised both of her hands. "You came to California to hurt me, Shaun. You said you were going to tell me at some point, but the part you don't understand is that if you had told me before I'd found out, it still would have hurt me. And you know why? Because you lied to me from the start." Tears filled my eyes.

"Don't, Jen. Please, don't cry. Fuck! You need to believe that I'm sorry."

I stared at him as he ran his hand through his hair while lowering his head. A few moments of silence passed.

"I do believe you're sorry."

"You do?" He looked up at me.

"Yeah. I do. And I know I've been a royal bitch, but I can't help it. It's how I have to be to protect myself and my heart. I know I've said it so many times, but you hurt me in ways I've never been hurt before."

"I know I hurt you, and I acknowledge your feelings, Jen.

It kills me knowing that I'm responsible for your pain. But I know there's a way we can work through it."

"And what if I don't want to, Shaun?"

"If that's how you really feel, then I have no choice but to accept it. But I want you to remember all the times we shared together. The laughter, the dinners, the days in bed, the walks on the beach, the sunsets, the shopping, the family gatherings, the things I've done for you, and the way I made you feel before I hurt you. I want you to remember how it was. Can you do that for me?"

I wanted nothing more than to go over to her and wipe away her tears, but I knew she didn't want that.

"I don't know." She brought her hand up to her face and wiped the tears from her eyes.

The elevator finally started to move.

"Thank God," she said as we both stood up.

When the doors opened, Sam and Stefan stood there staring at us.

"Oh my God. How long were you two in there?" Sam asked.

I glanced at my watch. "Over an hour."

"Damn elevator." Sam shook his head. "You okay, Jen?"

"I'm fine. Where's Julia?"

"Umm. She left. The girls were getting very cranky."

"Are you kidding me?" She sighed. "I have to go, but I am not getting back in that elevator." She turned and headed for the stairwell.

"Let's go into Sam's office," Stefan said.

I followed them in, and Sam shut the door.

"So, what's the problem with the condos?" I asked as I took a seat.

"Well—" Stefan gave me an odd look.

"There isn't a problem," Sam said.

My brows furrowed. "What do you mean?"

"How did it go with Jenni?" Stefan asked. "Did the two of you talk?"

"Oh, come on." I shook my head. "You didn't. Tell me you didn't."

They both looked at each other and didn't say a word.

"Listen, bro. You and Jenni needed to talk, and we knew she wouldn't spend one second in a room with you without leaving. So, we made sure she couldn't go anywhere," Stefan said.

"It was actually all Julia's idea," Sam spoke.

"She was never here, was she?" I asked.

"No. I drove her car to work."

"I cannot believe you two did that." I pointed at them.

"We told you we always have each other's backs." A smile crossed Stefan's face. "We look out for one another."

"And this was our way of looking out for the two of you," Sam said. "So, how did it go?"

"She told me she knows how sorry I am for what I did, but she doesn't want to work things out."

"Damn." Stefan shook his head. "She's more difficult than we thought."

"I told her I'd accept her decision, but she needs to remember all the time we spent together."

"Let me give you a piece of advice, bro," Sam spoke. "Leave her alone."

"What?" I frowned. "You two are the ones that put us in that elevator together and stopped it."

"I know, but now that you've talked and she has a clearer picture of how sorry you really are, it's time to back off. Trust me."

"Sam's right. The best thing you can do now is just to be a friend to her—no more talk about wanting her back, nothing. You need to rebuild your relationship as a friendship first. The rest will follow."

"How do you two know so much?"

Sam breathed out a laugh. "We've been through it already. And trust me, Julia and Jenni are alike. If Julia could come back to me after what I'd said to her, Jenni will come back to you."

"I hope so. Thanks, my brothers." I stood up and hugged them. "I appreciate everything you're doing."

CHAPTER 42

*J*enni

As soon as I got in my car, I called Julia.

"Jenni, oh my God! Are you okay?"

"I'm fine, sis. Did you eat yet?"

"No. I haven't had a chance."

"I'm going to get a carry-out for us from that Mediterranean place we love, and I'm coming over."

"Sounds good. I'll see you soon."

Before I pulled out of the parking lot, I called the order in. As I was on my way to pick it up, I called Wes.

"Hello, darling. How was lunch?"

"It didn't happen. I got stuck in the elevator for over an hour."

"Oh shit. Are you okay? Were you alone, or was it crowded?"

"I'm fine, and no, I wasn't alone. Shaun was in there with me. Just the two of us."

"OH! Sounds sexy. How did it go?"

"I'll fill you in tomorrow. I won't be back for the rest of the day. I'm bringing lunch to Julia's."

"Okay. If you need anything, call me. If I don't hear from you, I'll see you tomorrow."

"Thanks, Wes."

I picked up the food and pulled up to Julia's house. When I stepped through the sliding door, I set the bag on the island, and Julia walked into the kitchen.

"I just got the girls to sleep." She grinned.

"Aw, I wanted to play with them." I gave her a pout.

"Trust me. One of them will be up soon."

I reached into the bag and pulled out the food while Julia grabbed a couple of plates.

"How awful was it being stuck in that elevator?"

"It was horrible. There's no worse feeling in the world than feeling trapped."

"Were you alone or with a group of people?"

"You're never going to believe whom I was stuck with?"

Her brows furrowed. "Who?"

"Shaun."

"What?! What was he doing there?"

"I don't know. I guess Stefan called him and told him he needed him to come ASAP because there was an issue with the condos."

"Well, what happened? Did you ignore him?"

"No. We talked."

"Oh." Her brow raised. "And?"

"He just kept telling me how sorry he was, and he wants to work things out. I told him I knew he was sorry."

"Aw, so you finally forgave him?"

"Not really. I told him working things out wasn't what I wanted."

"I see. Now, who is the one lying?"

My brow furrowed. "Excuse me?"

"I know you still love him. Just like I still loved Sam after all that shit he put me through."

"I do love him, but it doesn't mean I want to be with him."

"Okay." She rolled her eyes.

"What is your problem, Julia?"

"You know what my problem is? It's you, Jenni." She voiced loudly.

"Wow, okay. Damn."

"You got hurt by that douchebag little boy when we were seventeen. First love, first crush, whatever. It set you on the path of relationship destruction. You turned to one-night stands, frequently, may I add, because that way there wasn't a risk of falling for someone. Then when you did meet someone who semi-piqued your interest, you dropped them like a hot potato because you only focused on all their faults. Then comes Shaun, and somehow and someway, you saw beyond his faults and only focused on the good in him. For the first time, you let your guard down and opened your heart to someone. Then you found out Shaun lied. Okay. A lie is a lie; I get it. But he had his reasons. And believe me when I say I don't think he'll ever lie again. If he didn't want you in his life, he would have walked away after you found out. He would have left you alone. Just the fact that he's telling you he loves you and wants to work things out means he's invested in you, Jen. If he were truly a cold-hearted bastard like you think he is, he wouldn't be doing the things he is to get your attention. Just think about that."

"Are you done now?"

"No. I'm not. "People make mistakes, and you, my darling twin, are not exempt. None of us are."

"I need some fresh air. Do you want to go down to the beach? You can bring the monitor."

"You go. I'll meet you down there."

I cleaned up from lunch and walked down to the beach to let the water sweep across my feet.

"Hi, Aunt Jenni." Lily ran over and hugged me.

"Hey, sweetheart. Why are you home from school already?"

"We had a half-day today."

"It seems like you always have half days."

"Yeah. I know. But I'm not mad about it." She grinned.

"I don't blame you, kid. I wouldn't be either."

"What's wrong?"

"Nothing, why?" I asked her.

"You look sad. Is it because of my Uncle Shaun? You have the same look my dad had when he and Alex stopped seeing each other."

"Maybe a little bit." I grabbed hold of her hand, and we started walking along the water.

"He's sad too, you know."

"Don't tell me you're defending him too." I glanced over at her.

"I don't know exactly what he did because ever since my parents found out that I overheard them talking about him being my uncle, they're extra careful now. It's so annoying."

I let out a laugh.

"But everyone deserves a second chance. I gave my mom a second chance, and I'm happy I did. You know why?"

"Why?"

"Because she really is a good person, and I know she loves me, and she's sorry for what she did. Her life was messy, and she couldn't handle it at the time. Nobody's perfect, and everyone makes mistakes. I'm sure you've made mistakes."

I stopped, knelt in front of her, and placed my hands around her arms.

"I have, and you are one special little girl." I pulled her into a hug.

"Thanks, Aunt Jenni."

"What's going on over here? Can I join the hugging party?" Julia smiled.

"Of course, Aunt Julia."

CHAPTER 43

*S*haun
    I stared out the window at Jenni and Lily down at the beach with a smile on my face. A while later, the sliding door opened, and Lily walked in.

"Well?" I asked her.

"I told her everyone deserves a second chance and that nobody's perfect and everybody makes mistakes."

"And?"

"I think I might have gotten through to her." She grinned.

"Good girl." I patted her head. "Are you ready for your fruit smoothie?"

"Yes! Can I help?"

"You sure can." I smiled.

The following day when I walked up to my office, I saw Jenni had taken down the black fabric, and my view of her office was open once again. She was in her office, and as much as I wanted to say good morning to her, I didn't. I pretended I didn't notice she took the cloth down and turned on my computer. While I was there checking the stocks and coordinating meetings for when I would be in New York, she walked into my office.

"Hey."

"Hi," I replied.

"Is this a bad time?"

"No. Not at all. What's up?"

"I have a meeting this afternoon with Seymour Klaus, the clothing buyer for Nordstrom."

"Nice." I nodded. "You must be excited."

"Excited, nervous, scared."

"Why are you scared?"

"What if he rejects me and my clothing line?"

"Well, he's obviously interested if he reached out to you for a meeting."

"I wanted to ask you—" She paused and looked down.

"Ask me what?"

"If you would go with me. I mean—it's your money that allowed me to develop this line fully. So, I thought maybe you would want to be there."

The corners of my mouth started to curve upward, and I instantly stopped them.

"Yeah. Sure. If you need me to go, I will," I spoke in a serious tone.

"Thanks. Um, don't take this as meaning anything."

"Like what?" I furrowed my brows at her.

"Anything other than business," she said.

"I don't. I haven't forgotten our little chat in the elevator."

My phone rang, and Adam was calling.

"If you'll excuse me, I need to take this. Hey, Adam, hold on a second. Jenni, what time is the meeting?"

"It's at one-thirty."

"Okay." I gave her a nod, and she walked out of my office.

J looked at the clock, and it was noon. Jenni had just walked back into her office from a meeting with the staff. Getting up, I walked over and lightly tapped on the door frame.

"Hey," she turned around and looked at me.

"Are we driving to the meeting together?"

"Um, I don't know."

"Well, if you want to, I'm heading out now and grabbing some lunch first on the way."

"Oh. I can just meet you at Seymour's office," she spoke.

"Okay. I'll see you there."

I was halfway down the hall when I heard her call my name.

"Shaun?"

"Yeah?" I turned around.

"I guess I'll go with you. I just have to grab my purse."

I silently smiled to myself.

She grabbed her purse, and we climbed into my car.

"Since we're meeting Seymour at Nordstrom, I thought it would be best to grab some lunch in that area."

"Yeah. Sounds good." She looked out the passenger window.

I could tell she was unsure about her decision to have lunch with me. I pulled up to the valet at The Grove and handed him the keys.

"Where do you want to go?" she asked.

"I'm in the mood for sushi, and I heard the Blue Ribbon Sushi Bar & Grill was good."

Suddenly, she grabbed hold of my arm and stopped.

"What's wrong?"

"If you want to go there, it's fine. But we have to eat at a table outside."

"Okay. A table outside it is."

When we approached the restaurant, Jenni stopped outside the door.

"I'll just wait here."

I furrowed my brows. "Okay."

"How can I help you?" A nice young girl smiled.

"An outside table for two, please."

"I'm sorry, but all of our outside tables are already reserved. I have a nice booth in the corner available."

"I'm afraid it has to be an outside table." I reached into my pocket and pulled out a one-hundred-dollar bill. "Perhaps, one is available?" I folded the bill and handed it to her.

"Silly me. There's one available. I don't know how I missed that." She grabbed two menus, and I followed her out the door where Jenni was.

"I got us a table."

"Thanks." A soft smile graced her face.

We took our seats and looked at the menus.

"What's going on with you?" I asked.

"What do you mean?"

"You wouldn't walk into the restaurant, and you said we had to sit outside. Why?"

"I had a bad experience here and haven't been back since."

"What happened?"

"I was having lunch with Grace, and a man walked into the restaurant with a gun and started shooting people. Grace made me get under the table while she grabbed her gun and went after him. She shot and killed him after he shot the manager."

"My God, Jenni. I had no idea. We can go somewhere else. I'm sorry."

"No. It's fine. The sushi is good. I just don't want to eat inside."

"That's totally understandable. Thank God you were with Grace."

"Yeah. I know. After calling 911, I called Simon, and he came right away. It was terrifying. Since then, I can't bring myself to step foot inside the place."

"I wish you would have told me."

The waitress walked over with our drinks and took our food order.

"I'm leaving for New York tomorrow," I said as I picked up my drink.

"For how long?"

"A couple of weeks at least."

"Oh. For business?"

"Yes. I have a couple of board meetings to attend, and other business needs my attention. I may be gone longer, but I'm not sure yet."

"Oh. Okay."

"So, if anything comes up, you can shoot me a text or call and let me know."

"Whatever comes up, I can handle myself. I would hate to bother you while you're putting out fires in New York." Her brow arched.

The corners of my mouth curved upward. "Ah, you're still living in the past, I see. One time, Jen. One time. And if you recall, we did a lot of hot Facetiming after that."

"I remember." She brought her glass up to her lips.

"Good." I smiled.

After we finished our sushi, we went to meet with Seymour. Jenni had already had pieces of her line delivered to him yesterday for him to view.

"Relax," I said as we took the escalator up.

"I can't. You don't understand. This is the first time anyone outside the family has seen my work. What if he hates it?"

"He's not going to. But if he does, he's an idiot, and I will have his job." I gave her a wink.

CHAPTER 44

*J*enni

"It's nice to make your acquaintance," Miss Benton.

"Please. Call me Jenni. This is Shaun Sterling. He's an investor for Simply Jenni."

"Mr. Sterling, it's a pleasure to meet you." Seymour extended his hand. "I know of your reputation back in New York."

"I'm not sure if that's a good thing or a bad thing." Shaun chuckled as he shook his hand.

"I think it's best I don't say." He smirked. Have a seat, please."

I looked over and saw my rack of clothing across the room. My heart was semi-racing, and the nervous feeling in my belly intensified.

"Let me start by saying welcome to the world of fashion. I'd done some research on you, and you were a high-end fashion model for years."

"Ever since I was eighteen." I smiled.

"Well, as far as I'm concerned, you nailed it as a fashion model, and you've nailed it as a fashion designer. I love your clothing line, and I would like to be the first person to jump on board the Simply Jenni trend and put your clothes in our Nordstrom stores across the world."

I wanted to jump up and scream, "YES." I wanted to throw my arms around Seymour and squeeze him tight. But that wouldn't be very professional.

"Thank you, Mr. Klaus. I'd love for Nordstrom to carry my clothing."

"Excellent. I'll get all the contracts drawn up and have them sent so you and Mr. Sterling can look them over. I'd also like to ask if you would be interested in designing an evening gown line exclusively for our stores only? Perhaps six to eight gowns?"

"Yes. Of course. I can do that."

"Hold on a second," Shaun said. "She can design a line of evening gowns, but not for your stores only. If she does that, you're basically hiring her to design exclusively for you."

"And?" Seymour's brow arched.

"She's not a Nordstrom designer, and Simply Jenni will not be exclusive to any one store. You're smart, Mr. Klaus, and I see what you're trying to do here. As long as my money is involved, it will not happen. So, my question is, do you still want a line of evening gowns?"

Seymour and Shaun both stared at each other for a moment. Neither one broke eye contact, and finally, I got to see him in business mode."

"Why don't we wait and see how the original clothing line sells first," Seymour said.

"That's fine. You can see her evening gown collection on her Instagram page as soon as it's complete. I look forward to looking over those contracts." Shaun stood up and extended his hand.

"Thank you, Mr. Klaus. I look forward to working with you." I smiled as I shook his hand.

I let out a deep breath as we left the store.

"Why did you do that?" I asked with an attitude.

"Isn't that why you wanted me to come? Did you really want a line of your evening gowns to be exclusive with Nordstrom? There's bigger fish out there, Jenni. Bigger fish who are going to jump at the chance for your designs. Never put all your eggs in one basket," he said as he handed the valet his ticket.

What he said made sense. I may not have trusted him as far as a relationship was concerned, but I did trust him in business.

He dropped me off at the curb of the studio.

"You're not coming in?" I asked.

"No. I'm going to go home and pack for my flight tomorrow, and then I'm hanging out with my brothers later since I won't be seeing them for a while."

"Oh. Okay. Where are you hanging at?"

"My house."

"I'm hanging with the girls tonight over at Alex's. If I don't see you, have a safe flight."

"Thanks. I will."

I opened the car door. "Thanks for coming with me."

"No problem." The corners of his mouth curved upward.

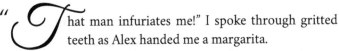

"That man infuriates me!" I spoke through gritted teeth as Alex handed me a margarita.

"I assume you're talking about Shaun?" She grinned.

"Who else? Nobody gets under my skin as much as that man does."

Julia let out a laugh.

"It's not funny, sis." I set my margarita down and took Lorelei from her arms.

"Actually, Jen, it is. What did he do now?"

"He's leaving for New York tomorrow," I said.

"Yeah. I know. That's why he infuriates you?" Her brows furrowed.

"No. I just didn't know if you knew. When did he tell you?" My eye narrowed.

"Last week."

"He told you last week, and he just told me today!"

"If you recall, you weren't speaking to him."

"Whatever. I'm over his dumb ass."

Alex laughed.

"I'm so confused here, Jenni. I thought you forgave him."

"Yeah, well, maybe I'm unforgiving him. We don't need no dumb guy, do we, baby?" I held Lorelei up. "No. No, we don't. Guys cause nothing but trouble."

"What are you telling our niece?" Stefan smirked as he stepped into the kitchen.

"Just that guys are dumb." I arched my brow.

"Oh. Okay." He smiled as he grabbed a bottle of scotch and walked back out.

~

*S*haun
My brothers and I sat outside in front of the fire pit with our guitars and waited for Stefan to come back with a brand-new bottle of scotch he had imported.

"Here it is." He handed it over to Sebastian.

"Nice. Let's open this baby up and see if she tastes as good as she looks." He grinned.

"When I walked into my kitchen, Jenni held Lorelei up and told her guys were dumb."

I let out a laugh.

"Any idea why she would say that?" Sam's brow arched.

"Who knows. I've been basically staying away from her."

"See!" Stefan pointed. "It's working. You're showing you don't care, and she doesn't like it."

"Yeah. It's all a game with these women," Sebastian said. "And don't any of you tell Emilia I said that."

"We did have lunch together today before the meeting with Seymour."

"Where did you go?" Sebastian asked.

"Blue Ribbon Sushi Bar & Grill."

"You got her to go there?" Simon asked.

"We had to sit outside. She wouldn't step foot in the restaurant. I had no idea what had happened when she and Grace went there."

"Yeah. It was scary for her. She hasn't gone back since. On the other hand, Grace wants to eat there all the time."

"Eat where?" Grace walked over and wrapped her arms around Simon's neck.

"Blue Ribbon Sushi Bar & Grill."

"Oh. I love that place. Ever since Jenni took me there, I've been obsessed. Anyway, we have to go." She kissed his cheek.

"Why?"

"I just got a call. There was a homicide over in Hollywood Hills."

"What the hell? I didn't get a call?"

"Have you checked your phone?"

He pulled his phone out of his pocket. "Oh. I guess I didn't hear it. Shit. Sorry, bros. Gotta run."

"No worries. You two have fun finding a killer," I said.

"I know I will." Grace grinned as she and Simon walked away.

As the evening ended and my brothers went home, I cleaned up and then went upstairs and climbed into bed. My flight was scheduled to leave at six forty-five a.m., and I had a long day ahead of me. I had hoped to see Jenni one last time before I left, but she never walked over, and I would miss her even more.

CHAPTER 45

*J*enni

"Not one word! Can you believe it?"

"Darling, what are you talking about?" Wes asked.

"Shaun! It's been a week, and I haven't heard one word from him."

"Is there a reason why you would?"

"No. But he still could have called or sent a text."

"There isn't a rule that says a guy has to text first. Send him a text message."

"No!" My brows furrowed. "He's probably too busy anyway."

"And I'm sure he's hitting the town at night. There's no way a man like Shaun Sterling stays locked up in his penthouse."

I stood there and narrowed my eyes at him.

"Sorry." He sighed. "Jen, what is going on? One minute you're talking how you can't stand him, and the next minute you're all pissed off because you haven't heard from him."

"He didn't even say goodbye." I slumped in my chair.

"Again, why would he? You made it very clear to the sexy man that you wanted nothing to do with him. Do you miss him?"

"No. I don't miss him!"

Wes breathed out a laugh.

"What was that for?"

"Even though you want nothing to do with him, it felt safe when he's here. Now that he's gone to New York, you can't handle him being gone."

"Not true." I sighed. "It's just rude that he didn't —"

My phone rang, and the name Sterling Capital appeared on the screen.

"Speak of the devil." Wes grinned. "Go ahead. Answer it."

I silently smiled as I pressed the answer button and put it on speaker.

"Hello."

"Hi. Is this Jenni?"

I glared at Wes as the knot in my belly tightened.

"Yes."

"It's Selena, Shaun's personal assistant."

"Oh. Hi, Selena." I stared at Wes.

"Shaun wanted me to let you know that he looked over the contracts from Seymour Klaus, and we're good to go."

"Great. He couldn't call me himself to tell me?"

"He's in back-to-back meetings all day. He asked me to call and tell you."

"Of course, he did."

"Excuse me?"

"Nothing. Thanks, Selena."

"You're welcome. Have a great day."

"You too."

I ended the call and inhaled a deep breath.

"That's right. Breathe. Breathe," Wes said.

~

"*H*e couldn't call and tell me himself?" I voiced loudly as I sat and had dinner with Simon and Grace at their house.

I was still all worked up from Selena's call earlier.

"He's busy, Jen," Simon said.

"That may be true, but it would have taken two seconds."

"Two seconds could cost him billions of dollars," Grace spoke.

"Really?" I cocked my head. "You two are taking his side?"

"There are no sides to be taken. You're the one who won't give him a second chance. So why should he call you? Maybe talking to you hurts too much still," Simon said.

"Wow. Wow." I nodded my head as I stared at him. "I feel like you need another bruise to match the other side of your face, detective."

Grace snickered.

"Just text or call him," Grace said as she reached over and placed her hand on mine.

"No. I will do no such thing. He's in for a rude awakening when he gets back. I'll tell you that."

"Really?" Simon's brow arched. "And what are you going to do?"

"Oh, you'll see." I pointed my fork at him. "Just you wait."

Simon let out a sigh. "I really don't want to have to arrest you, so keep it legal, please."

~

*S*haun
        I had just gotten home from the office and poured a scotch when my phone rang. Pulling it from my pocket, it was a Facetime call from Simon.

"Hey, bro. Good to see you." I grinned.

"Good to see you too. We had Jenni over for dinner tonight."

"How is she?"

"Pissed, bro. Pissed."

"Why?"

"Because you haven't bothered to text or call her, and you had your assistant call her."

I chuckled.

"She'll be okay."

"She threatened to bruise the other side of my face because she thought I was defending you."

I let out another chuckle.

"I'll be home in a few days, and I'll deal with her."

We ended the call, and I finished off my scotch. It was hard not calling or texting her. I missed her so much, but she needed to think I didn't care. I walked over to the couch, picked up my guitar, and started strumming. I just prayed to God that the plan I had worked out perfectly in my head worked when I got back to California and her."

CHAPTER 46

*J*enni

Today was going to be a good day. I was finally over Shaun and didn't give a shit anymore whether he called me or not. Screw him. Wouldn't he be surprised when he came home and found his shit moved all around? The thought gave me pure satisfaction. I'd forgotten that I still had his key, so I went over to his house the night I had dinner at Simon's to leave it. As I looked around his pristine place, I decided things needed to be rearranged, so I went at it. When I was finished, I left the key on the island, and when I left, I locked the door from the inside before shutting it.

"Good morning!" I brightly smiled at my staff as I entered the studio with a large coffee from Mojo Madness in my hand.

"You're in a good mood." Wes Grinned.

"I'm in a great mood."

"You must have talked to Shaun."

"Um, no."

"Then why are you in such a good mood?" His brows furrowed.

"Why not? The sun is shining, it's a beautiful day, I have five evening gowns designed and ready to be made, and my clothing line hits the Nordstrom stores in three months." I grinned. "Plus, I have a wonderful staff who loves me. They do love me, right?" I frowned.

"Of course, they do. We all love you." Wes hugged me.

"Excuse me? Are you Jenni Benton?" A man stood in the doorway of my office with a large bouquet of gorgeous flowers.

"Yes." I walked over to him.

"These are for you. I just need you to sign right here."

After I signed for the flowers, the man handed them to me.

"Thank you."

"You're welcome. Have a nice day."

"Those are gorgeous. I bet I know who they're from!" Wes grinned.

I opened the small envelope and pulled out the card.

"Miss me yet?"

I inhaled a sharp breath and slowly closed my eyes. He was not ruining my mood.

"What's that?" Wes said as he walked to the door.

"What's what?"

Suddenly, I heard the amplified strumming of a guitar coming from the first level. Walking out of my office and over to the railing, I looked down and saw Shaun sitting on a stool strumming his guitar. The moment our eyes met, he started singing the acoustic version of *Take on Me*. Everyone downstairs gathered in a circle around him as he sang, and his eyes never left mine. My heart pounded out of my chest, and tears filled my eyes as I listened to the sweet words that came from his mouth.

"If you don't forgive that man and go to him, I'm quitting," Wes said.

I walked down the stairs and over to him as he sang the last verse and strummed the final chord. He stood up from his stool and stared into my eyes. I had never loved him more than I did at that moment.

"You're an asshole." The corners of my mouth curved upward.

"I know I am. But I'm in love with you anyway." He smiled as he wiped the tears from my eyes.

I threw my arms around his neck and hugged him tightly.

"I missed you," I whispered in his ear.

"Not as much as I've missed you."

He broke our embrace and smashed his mouth into mine as my staff started clapping and whistling.

"Can you take the day off?" he asked.

"I can do anything you want me to." I grinned.

"You shouldn't have told me that." He smiled as he swooped down and picked me up.

"Miss Benton will not be in for the rest of the day." He announced to my staff. "Wes, grab her purse and bring it down."

As soon as Wes handed me my purse, Shaun carried me out of the studio and put me in his car.

"My place? It's a hell of a lot closer."

"Yes." I grinned, and then I remembered what I had done. "Oh, wait. Maybe that's not a good idea." I bit down on my bottom lip as I glanced over at him.

"What did you do?" a smirk crossed his lips.

"Nothing." I looked away.

"Jennifer?"

"Wow. You're using formal names now?" My brow arched.

He shook his head with a smile and took off in the direction of his house.

When we stepped inside, I gulped as he walked around.

"I see you did some redecorating while I was away."

"I was mad you didn't call or text me."

"I know you were." The corners of his mouth curved upward as he picked me up. "I guess I will have to make it up to you the best way I know how." He carried me up the stairs, and my legs tightened at the thought.

~

"*H*ow much did you miss this?" he asked as his tongue slipped up the inside of my thigh and stopped at my opening.

"So much." I gasped.

"And this?" His tongue circled me.

"Oh my God. So much." I gripped the sheets until my knuckles turned white.

His mouth explored me, and his finger dipped inside, bringing the ultimate orgasm on. I let out several pleasurable moans as my body shook with satisfaction. He slid his tongue up my torso and over my breasts before bringing his lips to mine. He thrust inside me, and I let out a puff of air at the feel of him. We went at it for a while and in different positions until he could no longer hold back. He exploded with one last thrust as he buried himself deep inside me. I smiled at the gratifying sounds that came from him as my nails dug into the flesh of his muscular back.

"I will never let you go," he whispered before his body collapsed on mine.

"Promise?"

"I promise," he spoke with bated breath. "I love you so much."

"I love you too, and I never stopped."

After our bodies calmed, we climbed into a hot bubble-filled tub, and he turned the jets on. Laying with my back against his chest, his arms tightened around me.

"We got this, Jen."

"Yeah. We got this." I tilted my head back and smiled at him.

"I heard you were a crabby little girl while I was gone."

"And who told you that?" I turned around in his arms and wrapped my legs around his waist.

"People." He grinned. "A lot of people."

"Well, maybe if you had called or texted, I wouldn't have been."

"I was giving you space."

"Maybe I didn't want you to."

"Somehow, I think you did." He smirked.

"I was just guarding my heart." I looked down.

He brought his finger under my chin and lifted it, so my eyes met his.

"You don't have to do that anymore because I'm never going to hurt you again. You have my word on that, Jenni."

"I know you won't." I brought my lips to his. "By the way, you haven't slept with anyone else, have you?"

His brows furrowed. "No. Of course not. Did you?" His brow raised.

"No. Why would I?"

"Why would I?"

"You were in New York. What did you do all that time?"

"I spent ninety-nine percent of it missing you."

"And the other one percent?"

"Taking over companies." The corners of my mouth curved upward.

"That's hot."

"Yeah? You like that?" He softly stroked my cheek.

"I do. You know, billionaires have always been my thing." I reached under the water and stroked his hard cock as my lips met his.

"Then it's a good thing I'm a billionaire." He let out a gasp.

CHAPTER 47

*S*haun

"There he is." Simon smiled and hugged me as Jenni and I stepped onto Sam and Julia's patio.

"Welcome home, bro." Sebastian, Stefan, and Sam all hugged me.

"Thanks. It's good to be home."

"Welcome home, son." My father patted my back as he held Nora.

"Thanks, Dad. May I?" I pointed to Nora.

"Of course. She is your sister." He smiled.

I took Nora from his arms and held her up.

"You have grown so much in the two weeks I was gone." I hugged her.

"I'm assuming things with Jenni are good," Sam said.

"Yeah, bro. Considering the two of you have been locked up in your house all day."

"We had much making up to do." I smiled.

"I bet you did." Simon grinned.

"Plus, I needed to put things back where they belong."

"What do you mean?" Sam asked.

"She took the liberty of messing some things up while I was gone."

Sam stood there and shook his head. "She's definitely Julia's sister. How bad was it?"

"Let's just say I wouldn't let her help clean up."

"Good man." He patted my back.

~

One Month Later

J was surfing with my brothers when we noticed our father staring at us from his patio. When we were finished, he called me over.

"Hey, Dad. What's up?"

"Sit down, son."

Celeste walked out and handed me a cup of coffee.

"Thanks, Celeste."

"You're welcome, Shaun." She smiled and went back inside.

"I wanted to talk to you about something."

"Sure. What is it?"

He handed me a large envelope. Opening it, I took out the papers inside, read them, and then stared at him.

"Dad, these are shares for Kind Design & Architecture."

"I know. They're your shares."

"I can't accept this."

"You can, and you will. That company belongs to you too, and you will have a seat on the board with your brothers."

"I don't know what to say. Thank you. This means a lot."

"You're welcome, son. I also wanted to discuss something else with you, and I would totally understand if you were opposed."

"What is it?"

"I was thinking that maybe you would be interested in changing your last name or adding to it."

"You want me to change my last name to Kind?"

"Shaun Sterling Kind. Shaun Kind Sterling. Whatever you want. You're a Kind, you're my fifth son, and you should carry the name that was rightfully yours to begin with."

"Yeah. I'll think about it."

"Okay. That's all I ask. Just give it some thought."

We talked some more, and after I finished my coffee, I went home.

"Hey." Jenni smiled when I stepped through the sliding door. "How was your surf?"

Walking over to her, I gripped her hips and kissed her.

"It was good. There were a lot of good waves today. My father called me over when we were done."

"Oh yeah? What did he want?"

"He gave me shares of the company and a seat on the Kind Design & Architecture board."

"Wow, Shaun. That's great." She grinned.

"Then he asked if I'd consider changing my last name to Kind."

"Say what?" Her brow arched. "Are you going to?"

"I don't know. I told him I'd think about it. There's something I need to tell you. I wanted to wait until everything was finalized."

"What is it?" she asked with worry in her voice.

"I'm moving Sterling Capital to California."

"What? Really?"

"Yeah. I don't want to keep going back and forth all the time. It's not like you can go with me because you're so busy with your company."

"What about your staff?"

"Adam is coming for sure, and so are some others. For

those that chose to stay back, I gave them a nice severance package. I also bought a private jet."

"Shut up!" She smiled as she slapped my chest. "You did not."

"I did. I figured we'd be using it all the time, traveling the world for fashion shows. Plus, the rest of the family can use it whenever needed."

"No more commercial airlines?"

"No more commercial airlines." I smiled as I kissed her lips.

"In that case, we have to plan a trip so we can test it out."

"Name a place, and we'll jet off to it. Anywhere you want to go."

"I'll get back to you on that." The corners of her mouth curved upward. "Have you found a building for Sterling Capital?"

"I'm in the process of looking. Do you know of any?"

"No. Maybe Sam and Stefan can build one for you."

"Hmm. That's not a bad idea. Did you make the bed?"

She stared at me as she chewed on her bottom lip.

"I'll take your silence as a no." I picked her up. "Since it's not made, I think we better put it to good use. What do you say?"

"I think you're brilliant, Mr. Sterling. Or is it Kind?" She grinned.

"You're cute." I carried her up the stairs and into the bedroom.

CHAPTER 48

ONE WEEK LATER

*J*enni

We were all at Sebastian's house having a barbecue. The guys were outside, and we girls were in the kitchen discussing wedding plans with Emilia.

"There's something I want to ask you," she said as she grabbed hold of my hands.

"Okay?"

"Will you be one of my maids of honors?"

"Oh my God! Yes. I'd love to!" I hugged her.

"Thank you. There was no way I could decide on just one person, so you're all my maids of honors. There's something else I want to ask you. Would you design the dresses along with my wedding dress?"

"What? You want me to design your wedding dress?"

"Yes. I want to walk down the aisle and marry the love of my life in a Simply Jenni couture."

"I literally can't breathe right now. I would be so honored to design your dress." I hugged her. "And ours."

"Thank you. I think we should celebrate. Sebastian

brought home a bottle of expensive champagne from the restaurant. Let's go outside."

The five of us went outside, and Emilia asked Sebastian to get the bottle of champagne.

"What are we celebrating?" Sam asked.

"Jenni is going to design my wedding dress and the maids of honors dresses."

"That's great, babe." Shaun held out his arms, and I took a seat on his lap. "I'm happy for you."

"Thank you." I kissed his lips.

Sebastian stepped out with the bottle of champagne, popped the cork, and poured each of us a glass.

"To Emilia and Sebastian on their upcoming nuptials," Simon said.

"And to Jenni. Who is going to make me look and feel like a princess." Emilia smiled.

"Cheers," Everyone spoke as we held up our glasses.

"Are you going to tell them?" I smiled at Shaun. "I think now is as good as any."

"Tell us what?" Simon asked.

"Yeah, bro. What secret are you hiding?" Stefan asked.

"Okay. Okay. Calm down. I'll let the cat out of the bag. I bought a private jet, and you all can use it whenever you need to fly somewhere. No more flying commercial."

"Shut the fuck up!" Stefan exclaimed. "You did not."

"I did." He grinned.

"That's my boy." His father smiled as he held up his glass.

"Between traveling to and from fashion shows, vacations, board meetings in New York, and other various things, it made sense."

"Wow," Sebastian said. "That is awesome. Thank you, my brother."

"You're welcome. There's something else." He pulled out the envelope next to the chair and handed it to Henry.

"What's this?" he asked.

"Open it and see."

I looked at Shaun and smiled as I softly kissed him.

Henry removed the paper and held it in his hand. I could see the tears swell in his eyes as he stared at it.

"Dad, what is it?" Sam asked.

"Yeah, Dad. What?" Simon spoke.

"It's a petition for a legal name change."

"Huh?" Stefan's brows furrowed.

"Your brother is changing his last name to Kind."

"Say what?" Sam smiled.

"Are you really?" Simon asked.

"Yeah. I'm changing it to Shaun Sterling Kind."

"That's terrific," Sebastian said. "That isn't going to screw up Sterling Capital, is it?"

"No. I'm not changing the name of the company. I'm just going to update the paperwork. But anything going forth will be under Shaun Sterling Kind."

Henry stood up and walked over to Shaun. I got up from his lap so he could stand up, and the two of them hugged.

"You have no idea how happy this makes me," Henry said. "Thank you."

"You're welcome, Dad. It was an easy decision."

CHAPTER 49

*S*haun

We went over to Jenni's apartment to grab a dress she wanted to wear to a party at the new Sterling Capital building in Los Angeles. As she was scouring her closet, I made myself comfortable on her bed.

"Move in with me," I said.

"What?" She turned and looked at me.

"Move in with me. You're already at my place ninety-nine percent of the time. If you had already been fully moved in, we wouldn't be here so you could look for your dress. It would already be hanging in the closet at my house."

"You never asked."

"I figured I'd come home one day, and all of your things would already be there. You'd say, 'Surprise! I moved in.' And when I do come every day and see that it hasn't happened, it makes me sad." I pouted.

She let out a laugh and climbed on top of me.

"I might mess up your place." She smiled.

"You already do." My lips formed a smirk.

"I'll make the bed if I'm the last one out of it when I feel like it. Perhaps, after my shower or my morning coffee."

"I'll make sure I'm the last one out of it."

"I'm not putting the cap back on the shampoo bottle after using it."

"You already don't."

"I won't be held responsible if my clothes don't quite make it into the laundry basket."

"Now that one is non-negotiable." My brow arched.

"I thought you'd never ask, you dork." The corners of her mouth curved upward.

"I didn't think I had to. But, Jenni, my love, will you please move in with me?"

"Yes." The beautiful smile that sat upon her lips widened. "I would love to move in with you."

"Excellent. The movers are coming Sunday morning to pack your things and move them to my house."

"What?"

"I knew you'd say yes, so I already arranged it. We'll spend all day tomorrow cleaning up and getting rid of the things you don't need."

"I need everything in this place." Her brow arched.

"Jen—"

"Okay, fine. There might be a few things I don't need."

"The first thing to go is that tattered nightshirt you wear."

"No." She frowned. "Not that."

"You no longer need it."

I reached under the bed, pulled out a white box with a red bow on top, and handed it to her.

"What is this?" She grinned.

"Open it and see."

She removed the lid and took out the soft baby pink, short-sleeved cotton nightshirt that said "I'm Shaun's" across the chest.

"Wow." She scrunched her nose at me, and I chuckled.

"Every time you wear it, you'll always remember the night I asked you to move in with me. No more sad night-shirts. Only happy ones. Or if you prefer, none at all." I grinned.

"I love it. Thank you." She leaned down and brought her lips to mine.

I couldn't help it, and I couldn't hold it in, so I laughed.

"What is so funny?"

"It's totally dumb. Are you really going to wear a night-shirt that says, 'I'm Shaun's?'"

"You bet I am. You bought it for me."

"As a joke. I didn't think you'd actually like it."

"I'm wearing it every single night."

"No, you're not."

"Yes, I am. EVERY. SINGLE. NIGHT!"

"Then I'll have no choice but to remove it from your body every single night."

"Promise?"

"You bet." I grinned as our lips met for a passionate kiss. "I love you, Jenni."

"I love you too, Shaun."

⁓

The car service I hired to take us to the party had arrived in the driveway.

"Jen, come on. The car is here," I shouted up the stairs.

"I'm coming. I was cleaning up the bathroom."

"Good girl." I kissed her forehead as she walked down the stairs. "You look stunning."

"Thank you. You look so handsome and yummy. Someone is getting lucky again tonight." She grinned.

"Stop. Do not get me worked up."

We climbed in the car, and the driver took us to the building where Sterling Capital was located.

"Wait. Why are we at the building where Kind Design & Architecture is?" Jenni asked.

"Surprise." I smiled.

"Sterling Capital is in the same building?"

"One floor down from Sam and Stefan."

"That's why you were being so sketchy about where your new office was located."

"I wasn't being sketchy. I wanted to surprise you."

"And the guys know about this?"

"Of course, they do. I told them not to mention it to you girls."

We walked into the building and took the elevator to the tenth floor. When the doors opened, the space was already packed with people. Waiters walked around with trays of delicious appetizers and glasses of champagne. There was also a bar with a bartender and a twelve-foot table filled with trays of cheeses, meats, vegetables, fruits, and desserts.

"Wow. This looks great," Jenni said as her arm was wrapped around mine.

"Selena did a great job. She would never have come if her fiancé didn't get that job promotion he wanted so badly."

"You had something to do with that, didn't you?"

"I will never tell." I gave her a wink.

I rounded up my family and had them follow me up the stairs to the second level. As we stood at the railing looking down at all my guests, I asked for everyone's attention.

"In a million years, I never thought I would leave New York, let alone move my company to Los Angeles. But these people right here, my family, are responsible for making that happen. Another person who is responsible is this woman right here." I grabbed hold of Jenni's hand. "The love of my life and the rising fashion designer of Simply Jenni, Jenni

Benton. I want to welcome my staff from New York and the additional new staff that just joined us here. May you all make me and yourselves a lot of money. I grinned. "Welcome to Sterling Capital." I held up my glass and nodded to the two men who removed the black cloth from the company name embedded on the wall in big gold letters.

"Congrats, bro." Simon grinned as he patted my back. "This is awesome."

"Thanks, Simon."

"It's good to have you one floor below," Sam said as he placed his hand on my shoulder.

"You'll love the building, bro. The café downstairs has delicious coffee. Uh, don't tell Julia I said that." Stefan smirked.

I let out a chuckle.

"I'm thrilled you stayed, and everything came together. Also, thanks for agreeing to be one of my best men at the wedding." Sebastian smiled. "It wouldn't feel right if all of my brothers didn't stand beside me."

"You're welcome, bro. Thanks for asking."

Everyone went back down to the first level, except me. I stood at the railing and looked down at my family, friends, and my new life. A life filled with love and surrounded by family.

"What are you doing up here?" Jenni asked with a smile as she hooked her arm around my waist.

"Just taking in everything I have to be grateful for." I wrapped my arm around her and pulled her into me.

"I'm going to miss you across the hall from me at the studio," she said. "I may have to find a new hot guy to put in there and stare at."

"He won't be as good in bed as I am." I gave her a wink.

"I'll let you know." She grinned.

"Have I told you how much I love you, Miss Benton?"

"Yes. But tell me again."

I cupped her chin in my hand. "I'm so in love with you."

"And I'm so in love with you." Our lips collided.

"Excuse me, Mr. Sterling?" A man interrupted us. "Would you mind giving us a quick interview?"

"Of course. And it's Kind. Shaun Sterling Kind." The corners of my mouth curved upward.

Thank you for reading Five of a Kind! I hope you enjoyed it.

To listen to the songs that inspired the story, click the link below for the playlist!

PLAYLIST

The Kind brothers' story isn't over yet. Join Sam, Stefan, Sebastian, Simon, Shaun, and their families as they continue to live their daily lives in book six of the Kind Brothers Series: The Kind Brothers.

PREORDER HERE

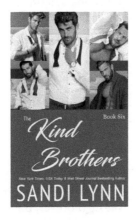

I want to invite you to join my Sandi's Romance Readers Facebook Group, where we talk about books, romance, and more! Come join the fun!

I'd love for you to join my romance tribe by following me on social media and subscribing to my newsletter to keep up with my new releases, sales, cover reveals, and more!

Newsletter
Website
Facebook
Instagram
Bookbub
Goodreads

Looking for more romance reads about billionaires, second chances and sports? Check out my other romance novels and escape to another world and from the daily grind of life – one book at a time.

Series:

Forever Series
Forever Black (Forever, Book 1)
Forever You (Forever, Book 2)
Forever Us (Forever, Book 3)

Being Julia (Forever, Book 4)
Collin (Forever, Book 5)
A Forever Family (Forever, Book 6)
A Forever Christmas (Holiday short story)

Wyatt Brothers
Love, Lust & A Millionaire (Wyatt Brothers, Book 1)
Love, Lust & Liam (Wyatt Brothers, Book 2)

A Millionaire's Love
Lie Next to Me (A Millionaire's Love, Book 1)
When I Lie with You (A Millionaire's Love, Book 2)

Happened Series
Then You Happened (Happened Series, Book 1)
Then We Happened (Happened Series, Book 2)

Redemption Series
Carter Grayson (Redemption Series, Book 1)
Chase Calloway (Redemption Series, Book 2)
Jamieson Finn (Redemption Series, Book 3)
Damien Prescott (Redemption Series, Book 4)

Interview Series

The Interview: New York & Los Angeles Part 1
The Interview: New York & Los Angeles Part 2

Love Series:
Love In Between (Love Series, Book 1)
The Upside of Love (Love Series, Book 2)

Wolfe Brothers
Elijah Wolfe (Wolfe Brothers, Book 1)
Nathan Wolfe (Wolfe Brothers, Book 2)
Mason Wolfe (Wolfe Brothers, Book 3)

Kind Brothers
One of a Kind
Two of a Kind
Three of a Kind
Four of a Kind
Five of a Kind

Standalone Books

The Billionaire's Christmas Baby
His Proposed Deal
The Secret He Holds
The Seduction of Alex Parker
Something About Lorelei

One Night in London
The Exception
Corporate Assets
A Beautiful Sight
The Negotiation
Defense
The Con Artist
#Delete
Behind His Lies
One Night in Paris
Perfectly You
The Escort
The Ring
The Donor
Rewind
Remembering You
When I'm With You
LOGAN (A Hockey Romance)
The Merger
Baby Drama
Unspoken
The Property Brokers